SQUACK is one of the ⟨...⟩ to provide design fee⟨...⟩ ductive. It decreases the subjective nature of most design discussions and allows us to create the best products for our customers.

– Larissa Scordato, Sr. UX Program
Manager, Design Ops at Amazon

I like how SQUACK shows the leader to be a human being who can make mistakes. This book eases people into the SQUACK feedback formula and shows how some of the easier feedback can be given with empathy and clarity. The more important feedback becomes clear and actionable.

– Tricia Adams,
Director at Expedia

Julie's SQUACK formula sticks with me daily. Coming from a non-tech role, it's been instrumental in helping me to grow my voice and advocate for solid design decisions with PMs.

– Caitlin Thakral,
Senior Content Designer at Uber

Gathering feedback and breaking group thinking has become more strategic thanks to the SQUACK method. As a UX Designer, I was able to find a way to innovate with a group of diverse, and often passionate practitioners because we had a shared way to frame our feedback.

– Kasia Wasko,
Product Designer at Amazon

SQUACK empowers everyone, especially the shy people on your team, to participate in feedback sessions because everyone has a common vocabulary. It's great to see a stakeholder classify their own feedback as a Suggestion instead of a deal-breaker. Plus, you'll be surprised how much it improves your ability to give feedback in important conversations at home.

– Kevin Dewey,
Product Designer at Pluralsight

SQUACK provides a scalable framework to collect feedback from stakeholders, regardless of their roles. This tool will save you time and energy, simplifying the intake process while increasing quality of feedback, virtually or in person.

– Akshara Chopra,
Product Designer

Data scientists need to collect feedback from other team members. We wrangle data, generate questions, form hypotheses, score our evidence, build a model, and rank our confidence. SQUACK simplifies our hacking process. Our algorithms, models, and dashboards can be SQUACKed like any design or product deliverable.

– Zoe Yang,
former Director of
Data Science at Capital One

Julie Jensen

SQUACK
TO IMPROVE FEEDBACK

The deceptively simple formula for hearing
and giving actionable, motivational, and
understandable feedback

SQUACK To Improve Feedback
The deceptively simple formula for hearing and giving actionable, motivational, and understandable feedback.

By Julie Jensen
Copyright 2021 Julie Jensen. All Rights Reserved.
Published by Rut Wrecker

Rut Wrecker is a publishing and consulting company that helps individuals and teams tackle mental hurdles that block their success, progress, or amusement. As the owner of the SQUACK trademark, Rut Wrecker, LLC, is the exclusive SQUACK licensee.
Contact licensing@rutwrecker.com for more information.

Book design and cover by Colleen Sheehan.

ISBN 978-1-7372049-0-9
Published in San Antonio, Tx

Library of Congress Control Number: 2021910471

See squackfeedback.com to order support materials, download worksheets, and discover the latest best practices.

Rut Wrecker
tackling mental hurdles

CONTENT

To the UX professionals who challenged and inspired me over the years. You taught me more than you know. I hope the SQUACK formula helps you collect feedback that motivates your craft, endurance, and grit.

FOREWORD

G et ready. You are about to soar.

The SQUACK feedback formula not only creates an opportunity ripe for puns, but it's also a deceptively simple and immensely effective concept that helps you understand, process, and appreciate feedback. This book is primarily focused on UX feedback, but here's the thing, no matter your personal, relationship, or work journeys, this book is going to help you.

These pages are filled with more than just theories and hypotheticals. Simply flip to any page and you'll find a no-nonsense, down-to-earth, common sense guide. A guide paired with real-world examples collected from Julie's broad variety of experience. And I mean very broad: a college computer center, the world's biggest software company, financial service companies, a top-secret nuclear research facility, the everything store, and even a prison. This range of perspectives forms the practical hands-on tips that will help you engage with partners, stakeholders, and managers.

Imagine engaging with passionate, smart, confident stakeholders in a stuffy conference room. They all support doing the right thing for our customers, but they disagree about how to get the job done. One stakeholder in particular voices opinions with such strong conviction, they are often interpreted as do-or -die mandates.

I prepared to present our team's design, waiting for decimating comments. But, I prefaced the meeting with an introduction to SQUACK. As I collected the feedback, it became clear none were Critical elements that had to be addressed. They were simply Suggestions derived from the stakeholders' passion and perspective.

Our UX team has fully adopted this feedback model; even incorporating it into our digital collaboration tools. Everyone, including the stickler stakeholders have flocked to categorizing their feedback using SQUACK. The UX team deciphers action items quickly based on the color of the digital notes and the labelling of the comments.

In another high-stress moment, I've collected many volumes worth of feedback getting my thesis proposal approved by the Internal Research Board, the chair and the committee members. By applying SQUACK to my personal work in this academic setting, I've been able to address the pivotal parts of the thesis. I've focused and saved countless hours of having my nose stuffed in a book instead of doing the things that really impact my work: talking with people and hearing their stories. You may not think to apply a work-related technique to your personal life, but SQUACK breaks the barriers. It works in any situation where people are sharing their ideas, expressing their opinions, and striving to persuade you.

Of course, knowing that SQUACK is pronounced squawk in the Pacific Northwest and squaaack in Texas; I suggest everyone try out their Texan drawl.

David Scaliatine,
Head of Design
Frost Bank

PREFACE

THE 100-WORD CHALLENGE

AND A 26% SURPLUS

Ah, the dreaded feedback session. You worry, despite your confidence, that your stakeholders will shred your deliverable with stray ideas and bewildering comments. They may chirp complaints, cluck for additional user data (swearing they need evidence), and screech about reducing costs. All their swearing can sound more like squawking caged birds than hyper focused professionals.

They expect you, as a designer, researcher, or writer, to juggle their feedback, understand expectations, decipher constraints, and meet business and technical needs. It's your responsibility to filter through all the noise to find the salient valuable ways to improve. But knowing precisely *how* to fix the design tends to be a frustrating trial-and-error exercise.

After a particularly hurtful and nearly hazardous feedback session about our team's design for a mobile app, I knew I needed to search for best practices for giving and receiving feedback. I knew our stakeholders did not intend to confuse or demoralize the team. The feedback didn't need to reflect any expertise about the art and science of design; the stakeholders simply needed a better way to share their ideas constructively.

When I searched for a method to clarify feedback, I suffocated through a maze of twists, turns, and dead ends. Amazon alone maxed out at 5,000 books about feedback and Google offered more than 621 million search results.

To combat this deluge of feedback advice, I challenged myself to create a 100-word solution that would close the gap between what our stakeholders say and what the design team hears.

And that's SQUACK: a 74-word formula for feedback.

Yep, 74 words.

Go ahead and read it on page 2. Use it. Share it with your team. Then, SQUACK back to me about how it works for you and how you've tweaked it at julie@squackfeedback.com.

Yes, it took me nearly 200 pages to describe a 74-word formula. Guilty. But within that description, I include stories to help you harness the power of SQUACK.

As of this writing, I have a series of three SQUACK books. This book is intended for UXers, who hear feedback from a variety of stakeholders and managers. Consequently, it provides best practices for role modelling SQUACK, understanding stakeholders, and acting on feedback. *SQUACK to Nurture a Collaborative Culture* is intended for executives and stakeholders who want to create a healthy culture where constructive criticism is welcomed across disciplines. *SQUACK to Empower Your Team* is written for design managers who act as a liaison between stakeholders and the UX team. If you're the only UXer in your company, you may benefit from both this book and the UX manager version, particularly the chapter about hatching SQUACK on a team.

As the title says, SQUACK is *deceptively simple*. You can start using it with your stakeholders and peers today and then refer to the best practices in this book to help you hone the formula.

THE SQUACK
FEEDBACK FORMULA

Categorize your feedback accordingly:

Suggestion

A comment or idea based on opinions or personal experiences.

Question

An area that needs clarity or exploration.

User Signal

Data, feedback, or research that spurs a compelling Suggestion or authentic Kudo.

A   C   K

Accident

A typo, copy and paste error, misalignment, or math mistake.

Critical

A problem that must be resolved because of the potential business risk or customer pain.

Kudos

Praise or gratitude.

3

INTRODUCTION

We all crave a five-star review and never want to hear our stakeholders complain: "What happened to my feedback? I don't see the changes I requested!"

We may avoid changing our designs if our stakeholders sound like screeching, squalling, and chirping birds. SQUACK helps UXers decipher those random squawks that are shared during design reviews and it's more effective than calling stakeholders a loon or dodo bird (as tempting as that is, especially during unruly feedback sessions).

The SQUACK feedback formula enables you, the feedback recipient, to understand and prioritize what you hear.

You will likely need to role model the SQUACK formula for your stakeholders. You may need to find sympathetic and influential stakeholders to help you hatch the formula across your team. And you may discover that your stakeholders resist giving frontline experts much ownership and decision-making authority. Several resources at squackfeedback.com can help you wade through these change management challenges and emerge clean and unscathed on the other side of the feedback swamp.

I have coached employees and managers from Amazon, Uber, Microsoft, Google, Facebook, Expedia, and other organizations to use SQUACK during their design reviews. SQUACK works because it gives feedback providers and receivers a common language and prioritization formula.

Designers and other makers, including content creators, business analysts, artists, presentation authors, dashboard crafters, animators, bloggers, photographers, storyboarders, and algorithm architects, may feel vulnerable when exposing your deliverables for feedback. Well-intentioned stakeholders may not understand that makers simply can't react to all their opinions, especially when they're slaving to meet aggressive deadlines and working under nearly impossible constraints.

Designers want to create exemplary experiences that not only exceed stakeholder expectations but also earn lavish customer attention.

SQUACK muzzles the noise.

Why Did I Write This Book?

Admittedly, I haven't created prototypes, conducted usability tests, or written UI text in years. Despite lacking recent hands-on-the-keyboard experience, I have coached, mentored, and led UX teams for 20+ years. And I'm observant.

I've seen and heard makers of all kinds struggle to get actionable feedback from their partners, managers, and stakeholders. I recognize their frustration, persistence, and talent.

The SQUACK formula, and this book, are my opportunity to give back and pay forward. I appreciate the people I've worked among who spurred challenges, gratification, and laughter throughout my career. My hope is that this book will help you live up to the expectations and opportunities you have for yourself and your team so that you can appreciate your accomplishments in solving every UX challenge.

By the way, if you're reading all three SQUACK books, you may think I have multiple personalities.

I really don't.

I've just donned numerous hats, appreciated various viewpoints, and grown my perspective. I hope your viewpoint expands throughout your career too, so you can SQUACK as a UXer, a design manager, and an executive stakeholder.

Who Should Use SQUACK?

Any maker can benefit from SQUACK. Seriously. The people who create documents, decks, dashboards, designs—anything intended for someone else to consume—can use SQUACK to collect, understand, and act on feedback.

I use SQUACK every day, up to the executive level, down to the entry level, and across the organization: analytics, content, data science, design, engineering, marketing, operations, product, program, research, and strategy teams.

Although I created SQUACK to distinguish noise from action items during design critiques, I've SQUACKed during an assortment of discussions. The team has asked people to SQUACK when reviewing our annual strategic plan, creating algorithms, conducting sprint retros, reviewing business KPIs, and brainstorming marketing campaigns.

I have also written my employees' annual performance reviews with Suggestions, Critical improvements, User Signal from their peers, and Kudos as congratulations.

Anything you create using software or your hands is a deliverable.

Your deliverables are crucial for the organization to explain, align, plan, drive, and deliver. Actionable feedback across disciplines, levels, teams, and silos enables the best deliverables.

SQUACK makes feedback clear and actionable.

Throughout this book, I generically refer to the maker's work as a deliverable. That deliverable can vary from a research plan, a low-fidelity wireframe, a description of an algorithm, or a spreadsheet to a pixel-perfect application, an infographic, a data visualization, a dashboard ... the list goes on.

Why Should You Use SQUACK?

I have seen SQUACK improve our critique processes across multiple disciplines, prevent us from fixating on careless errors, untangle opinions from risks, encourage shy employees to find their voice, promote collective accountability for Critical requirements, and encourage people up and down the hierarchy to feel empowered. The best practices and real-life examples throughout this book are intended to help you harness these benefits.

One more reason to use SQUACK—because it's fun. In "Making Good Citizenship Fun," an Opinion piece published in the New York Times in February 2012, behavioral economist Richard Thaler wrote: "As every successful parent learns, one way to encourage good behavior, from room-cleaning to tooth-brushing, is to make it fun. Not surprisingly, the same principle applies to adults. Adults like to have fun, too."

When our fun-seeking cross-disciplinary team at Capital One conducted SQUACK sessions, we'd throw a rubber chicken around the conference room. The chicken would squawk each time one of us launched it to someone else sitting at the table, reminding us not to take ourselves too seriously.

You can toss a squawking rubber chicken around the room (or have all the attendees squeak their chicken over a conference call) when someone drifts into a lengthy opinion instead of following the Suggestion formula (see page 33 for details), when each person has finished giving your SQUACK feedback to signal the next person to start, or when you agree with another SQUACKer's comments. Or, even better, create your own reason to squawk or throw the chicken, based on your team's culture and ceremonies.

Even figuring out how to pronounce SQUACK can be fun. Tech teams in Washington tend to pronounce it "squawk" (as in *hawk*), and financial services teams in Texas pronounce it "squaaack" (as in *quack*). Meanwhile, folks on the East Coast say "squuck" (as in *duck*).

Regardless of how your team pronounces SQUACK, we all work hard on our deliverables. Receiving and giving feedback to improve ourselves and our work should be fun and elevating, not deflating or stifling. So, let's seek opportunities to laugh at ourselves and SQUACK at one another.

How Did SQUACK Hatch?

The idea for SQUACK started when I dreamed about acting on a sitcom, expanded when I taught journalism to prisoners, and evolved over my 20+ year career as a UX manager in retail (Amazon), technology (Microsoft), and financial services (Capital One, USAA). Each company presented a distinct relationship between the feedback provider and the recipient, which exposed the best practices I describe throughout this book.

The origin of the formula did not follow the mnemonic spelling. It started with *S* for Suggestion and then *K* for Kudos. I rearranged the categories to form the memorable and fun word *SQUACK* when I gave myself the 100-word challenge. Each category strengthens the others, and together they provide a holistic feedback formula, stronger united than separate.

Here are the origin stories for each category, in the order I generated them.

The letter *S*, for Suggestion, stemmed, improbably, from an episode of *The Facts of Life* in which Blair, the snob, appoints herself as a special education teacher for a gorgeous male student. Despite the warnings about his special needs from Mrs. Garrett, the housemother at the all-girls boarding school, Blair arrogantly proceeds to instruct him in art appreciation and painting. She aims to expand his natural talent and predictably loses her patience as he struggles to understand the artistic concept of perspective. She yells and orders him to paint "Bolder! Bolder!"

This 1982 episode, "Different Drummer," would offend us deeply today. Every character mocked the man with degrading labels. Yet, the episode spurred my young imagination. I wondered how I would respond if an art teacher yelled at me to paint "bolder." If I didn't know what she meant by "bolder," how could a special-needs student correctly interpret her instruction?

I would have a few choice words for any teacher who yelled at me.

I imagined elbowing Blair away and telling the young man, "Remember, we want to make the item feel close to us. So, it needs to appear bigger;

like when you hold your hand close to your eyes, it looks bigger than when your hand rests on your desk. Let's make it look bigger by using a larger brush to paint a line that is at least a half-inch thick." I knew my script would sound less snooty, less arrogant, and less dictatorial. The artist needed to know how to be "right," not just "bolder."

I never expected I would hear professional "Blairs" throughout my career demand bolder, braver, and brighter designs. Yet I have heard exactly that. They may not call anyone on the team derogatory names, but their demands can still degrade and bewilder.

My role playing provoked the *S* for Suggestion in SQUACK, which today helps translate opinions ("Make it bolder") into actionable feedback ("Use a half-inch brush because you need it to appear bigger").

The letter *K*, for Kudos, surfaced when the inmates I was teaching at a local prison revealed the importance of promoting positive patterns. The prisoners, who earned the opportunity to join the journalism class based on their good behavior, wrote and published their own newspaper, *The Rap Sheet*.

Attending the journalism class helped the prisoners escape loneliness. They met as a group, discussed the article submissions, and shared creative control. They felt empowered.

I felt empowered, too. As I started this first professional job, I radiated idealism. I wanted crisp headlines, worthy stories (important to our readers and not ourselves), perfect grammar, and a well-orchestrated production process to predictably distribute the newspaper within the prison. I expected to trim, axe, or hack the prisoners' writing to fit within the columns of the newspaper.

My expectations devastatingly failed to align with reality.

People behind bars tend to think in months or years, depending on when they are up for parole. They don't think in terms of the daily or weekly deadlines required to edit stories, design pages, and print and distribute a newspaper.

The prisoners were notorious for ignoring deadlines.

They ignored the 4 ws and 1 h of writing an engaging article—quickly answer who, what, when, where, why, and how. Instead, they wrote superfluous details that their readers didn't *need-to-know*.

So, here I was, standing alone at the front of the class, a class that was full of prisoners in gray uniforms (worn by those convicted of misdemeanors like theft and assault), blue uniforms (worn by the white-collar criminals), and, on occasion but more frequently than I liked, orange jumpsuits (worn by those convicted of violent felonies like rape and murder).

I switched tactics.

I decided to persuade through positive reinforcement rather than demands or academic expectations. I knew the journalism best practices, but I needed to convey Kudos cordially and convincingly. I needed to empathize with their constraints, not force them to align to my goals. *The Rap Sheet* was, after all, being published by the prisoners for the prisoners.

So, when they began adjusting to the deadlines and organizing their content, I congratulated them. During each class, we examined what worked for our readers— the other prisoners, the guards, the warden, and the parole board members. Over time, we met our print deadlines and produced the newspaper at a predictable cadence.

SQUACK uses Kudos to thank people and reinforce best practices across teams and individuals alike.

∧

The letter *A*, for ∧ccident, emerged when an editor crushed my pride at the University of New Mexico. As a writer for our campus computer labs, part of my job included integrating dozens of how-to articles into one comprehensive document. The terminology across the documents bled chaos, as though each writer lacked awareness of the others. In fact, they did. Multiple students wrote the articles over multiple years without any concern for consistency.

I tamed the mess by spreading index cards all over my desk, and several other flat surfaces: the bookcase, the chairs, the windowsill. The concepts on each card defied any rational organization.

Admittedly, I took pride in the final document. No desktop publishing; no out-of-box templates. Just immature word processors. Pretty prehistoric. Frankly, it was a feat.

And I got paid to do it. Ahhhmazing.

As a student employee, I had access to the secure stockroom for work-related printing, color paper, and oversize staplers. I lingered by the printer one Friday evening for 40 minutes watching it process my compiled document. Alone. Crossing my fingers.

Please, no paper jams.

Please, no skipped pages.

Please, no smeared ink.

Yay! It printed without any defects.

I couldn't enjoy my achievement for long. The editor returned my printed document on Monday with scratches, scrawls, and corrections written in blood-red ink, on every.single.page. I felt failure seep through my eye sockets straight into my veins as I agonized about leaving so many mistakes. I tucked the tainted work into my backpack and went home. Dejected.

When I returned to the lab on Tuesday, I took 10 deep breaths and responded. I graciously thanked the editor: "I saw in your edits that I should've condensed *electronic mail* to *e-mail* instead of *email*. If something like this happens again, feel free to just note the mistake the first time it appears. Then you won't have to spend your time and energy looking for an error that I can easily correct using Find & Replace."

Within SQUACK, the *A* reminds feedback providers to discreetly identify Accidents, rather than blatantly announcing them and potentially humiliating the person who made the errors.

• • •

The letter *U*, for Ʋser Signal, sprouted from creating the user research discipline at USAA, a Fortune 200 financial services company renowned for its customer service ("member service," in USAA parlance). The team initiated a full spectrum of research activities to collect Ʋser Signal that uncovered members' likes, expectations, worries, thoughts, and feelings. We identified user success criteria and measured our digital tools, paper forms, phone calls, and every member interaction against those criteria. Aligning to Ʋser Signal became part of USAA's DNA. We proudly celebrated when we launched a new product or improved an existing experience, because we knew members would be enthusiastic as well.

Although we focused primarily on understanding our members, we also ensured that internal tools met employees' expectations. The employees who answered the phones and helped our members had a pretty dreary set of tools, mostly antiquated monochrome terminals (literally green-on-black screens) with keyboard interfaces (no scroll pad, no touch screen, no tapping). The phone agents tabbed through numerous tedious and unattractive screens.

Except for one interface.

When an agent needed to transfer a member to another agent, they located the phone number via a map of the United States. The agents actually liked this tool. It was their eye candy. As we overhauled all the internal tools, we knew changing this interface would contradict the employees' wants. For the first time, we would need to veer from our User Signal.

We anticipated significant backlash from the agents. We needed to explain why we were eliminating the attractive map. We measured how long it took to find a phone number using our new form-based design versus the map interface. Our new design proved to be undeniably faster and more accurate, but it was much less attractive. To help with the change management, we shared our evidence with the agents.

To train them on the new tool, we recorded an agent transferring a call, first using the map and then using our new search tool. We used a large stopwatch to show the amount of time that elapsed from answering to transferring the call. The clock ticked away on both designs side by side. With proof that our redesign would increase their efficiency the agents accepted the change, a bit begrudgingly but justifiably. They appreciated the proof.

Within SQUACK, User Signal provides evidence for Kudos when we proudly align to user needs and Suggestions if we veer from them, including potential ways to explain our decisions.

?

The letter *Q*, for Question, required two paths: one to reveal how to ask questions and the other to expose how to answer them.

As a journalist, I had learned best practices for asking questions. To build rapport with a source, I started with simple, no-brainer questions. I knew if I could get them comfortably answering the filler questions, they'd divulge truly quote-worthy news when I blurted a candid question that jabbed at the real story.

When I used their answers in my article, I balanced my *want-to-tell* against my readers' *need-to-know*. I *wanted* to share the tedious details about how I clawed through raw data, interviewed multiple people, and unburied the truth; but my readers just *needed* the truth.

They didn't care about all my tedious work.

That realization foreshadowed how I learned the importance of answering questions as a UX manager, especially during design reviews with Microsoft executives. Just like my sources for journalism articles, designers tended to unintentionally reveal the WARTS (weaknesses, adaptations, risks, tradeoffs, and shortcomings) about our work. This tended to erode trust because, although we *wanted* to explain the entire story behind the design, the executives just *needed* to make business decisions.

Microsoft executives practiced Precision Questioning/Precision Answering that emphasized asking broad questions and then drilling down with increasingly detailed questions. Although the drill-down often felt like an interrogation, the process focused squarely on the user. In this case, the users were the stakeholders asking the Questions. They comprised our entire audience for the design review.

We had to build rapport—answer the Question being asked, first and foremost. Because stakeholders tend to focus on the business requirements and technical capabilities, the UX team needed to as well. At least initially. Eventually, we extended the aperture to describe the design implications too.

Within SQUACK, Questions are clearly worded and answered. SQUACK helps the feedback recipients recognize that their user is the feedback provider, whose expectations need to be understood and met.

The letter *C*. for **Critical,** originated when the product team aimed to disrupt our industry. We needed to ensure that all our experiences met legal and compliance requirements—that the experiences were "unassailable" in legal parlance. So, we hired three times as many lawyers as designers.

During our reviews, the design team passed printed screenshots from one lawyer to another. We discovered that sometimes legal opinions varied. The designers needed to distinguish the opinions from the risks. So, we asked our legal partners to use an *S* to identify a Suggestion based on their opinion and a *C* to identify a Critical compliance issue. We often listened as the lawyers deferred to one another's expertise.

When asked about her experience, one of our compliance experts, reflected: "Distinguishing our personal opinion from legal opinion was eye-opening and insightful. I, personally, became a better critic of actual design by listening to the others and reflecting on my words as we tried to persuade the product team to make changes based on what we liked versus what caused an actual legal risk."

Beyond legal risks, SQUACK identifies other Critical issues, including brand misalignments, strategy failures, and harm to either the business or our customers.

How Should You Use This Book?

First, let me describe the three books in the series. Each book tailors SQUACK for a typical audience within the UX life cycle.

SQUACK to Improve Feedback: The deceptively simple formula for hearing and giving actionable, motivational, and understandable feedback. For UX designers, researchers, and writers who create experiences for other people and hear feedback from stakeholders, managers, executives, lawyers, and other professionals.

SQUACK to Empower Your Team: The clever formula for translating feedback so that your UX team remains confident, effective, and motivated. This version details best practices for hatching SQUACK within an organization, including tools to humorously consider who should lead the change efforts to adopt SQUACK, ensure that teams use SQUACK before they can resist, and mold the approach for face-to-face or remote sessions.

SQUACK to Nurture a Collaborative Culture: The savvy resource for spurring teamwork, amplifying diverse voices, and transforming feedback across disciplines. For executives and stakeholders who want to create and nurture a strong critique culture and embrace servant leadership. This version describes the power and process of SQUACKing across disciplines and deliverables.

As a UX professional, read the SQUACK formula on page 2 and practice using it on a website or mobile app you despise. You'll likely have plenty of advice for that app's designers, and SQUACK can help you formulate clear, concise, and constructive feedback for them. Then you can use SQUACK during an upcoming design review or critique with your peers or stakeholders.

The remainder of this book will help you further hone your SQUACKing expertise. The section "Understanding and Using SQUACK," provides definitions, formulas, and best practices for hearing feedback. The section "Let SQUACK Take Flight on Your Team," provides advice for planning, facilitating, and acting after the SQUACK sessions.

Incidentally, I emphasize my UX background by collectively referencing research and writing deliverables within design. If you are not a traditional UXer, I invite you to substitute your own work for *deliverable* or *design* and then share how SQUACK works for your discipline by reaching out to me at julie@squackfeedback.com.

The book's Conclusion, "Oh, the Places You'll SQUACK," spurs you to accept a couple of challenges and seek other assets (posters, training, and other educational tools) to help your team hatch SQUACK.

Throughout the book, I've included the *In real life* stories to reveal examples about myself, my choices, and my past or the selves, choices, and pasts of people I care about. Sometimes I use real names and other times I protect people's feelings with fictitious names. *Ima Ginary*, *Jun Ior*, *Em Bellisher*, and *Bo Gus* are fictional names based on real UXers. *Fran Tic*, *Egoma Naic*, *Deni Er*, and *Ami Cable* are fictional names based on real stakeholders. These anecdotes are meant for you to laugh, grow, and expand your expertise. And they may remind you that your colleagues and stakeholders are *just* human too.

Remember that requesting and giving feedback should be fun. You've worked hard to make that deliverable. So, answer others' Questions, consider their Suggestions, remember the Kudos, and take action on any Accidents and Critical comments.

If you're giving feedback, enjoy the opportunity. Formulate Suggestions, ask Questions, and convey authentic Kudos. Show that you're interested in the other person's work. Feedback is a gift that should be given freely, with no obligation to accept.

Let the SQUACKing begin!

UNDERSTANDING & USING SQUACK

I love the annual postings of the "world's worst web designs," with their garish screenshots, blunt descriptions, and mocking advice. The critiques are great examples of nonactionable, nonspecific, and non-nice opinions. I am happy that none of my designs has been mocked on a "world's worst" list—at least not that I'm aware of.

As an exercise, let's dissect a critique of a design from the preceding century and reformulate the feedback using SQUACK. Emily Grace Adiseshiah wrote an entertaining review of Disney.com with, admittedly, little respect for the designers who did the work.

Although these "world's worst" lists are presumably meant for entertainment, her comments echo feedback I've actually heard about our team's designs.

The left side of the next page depicts the original critique from justinmind.com* ... The right side shows the same critique using SQUACK. The circled numbers represent sticky notes if the SQUACK session happened in person or notes from digital tools if the session occurred remotely.

---

* https://www.justinmind.com/blog/10-90s-websites-designs-you-wont-believe-existed

90s website fails

... The 1996 Disney site.

We're drawn to the site's double bottom navigation system—a must-have navigation system for 90s websites. On the one hand you've got your whimsical wave of navigation links. On the other, you've got your bottom navigation bar, which looks a little odd with its links displayed in that brown/maroon color.

Disney also seems to have gone all out on fonts in the 90s, employing over six different fonts just for the Homepage!

And yes, we are the logo police. Check out poor Mickey Mouse!

Phew. The original review was pretty scathing. Let's re-write the critique using SQUACK.

Here's what the notes would say in this example SQUACK session. The circled numbers represent sticky notes if the SQUACK happened in person or notes from digital tools if the SQUACK occurred remotely.

① C: "We need to fix the Mickey Mouse logo to match the brand Disney has built for 70+ years and make sure the logo lockup is accessible. The web-optimized logos and images are available from... ."

② S: "To increase the legibility of the page, let's eliminate fonts that are difficult to read. Eliminating 'Table of Contents' and removing the wave of navigation links will help. I suggest eliminating a couple more fonts for even better legibility."

③ S: "Because the page has so many redundant links (the whimsical wave of navigation links duplicates the links in brown/maroon), let's remove the links in the wave. The remaining links, which are not part of the image, will be easier for screen readers to identify, which will enable visually impaired customers to use the site as well."

④ S: "Since customers may struggle to identify the brown/maroon color as a link, let's take advantage of the industry standard: links should be underlined blue text."

The letters represent a few more SQUACK comments that were not included in the original critique.

Ⓐ Q: "What happens when users tap on 'Where Merry Magic Is in the Air,' 'Log on Sunday for the $5000.00 Drawing,' and 'Watch the ABC Sunday Night Movie'?

Ⓑ K: "Kudos for showcasing Disney's three business areas—Travel, Movies, and Television—with an iconic image of Mickey and an image from 101 Dalmatians."

Ⓒ Q: "What did the usability participants expect when they selected the 'Fun' link and how well did we deliver on their expectations?"

D S: "To enhance consistency, let's list the links in the same order as the images (the 'Travel,' 'Movies,' and 'Television' images and links should appear in the same order). Ideally, we should list them in order of revenue, frequency, or some other metric important to Disney."

The rewritten and augmented SQUACK comments reinforce that the reviewer and designer share the same goals and emphasize that the intent is to improve the site (not merely make fun of it).

How does the SQUACK review affect your approach to the redesign versus the original mocking critique? What would your redesign look like based on the SQUACK review versus the mocking critique?

S FOR SUGGESTIONS

Definition: A comment or idea based on opinions or personal experience.

Formula:

$$\left\{ \begin{array}{c} \text{do this} \\ + \\ \text{explain why} \end{array} \right\}$$

Color: Yellow represents delightful sunshine as you hear ideas to improve your work. Most of your joy comes from knowing the Suggestions are not meant to infuriate, humiliate, or irritate you. Rather, they are meant to elevate your work.

Symbol: ∼ The tilde indicates an approximation because you get to evaluate the merits of the Suggestion. As long as you communicate your decisions and actions after the SQUACK session, the choice to act is yours.

Ask Questions to ensure that you understand their Suggestions.

When Suggestions seem irrelevant, ask Questions to understand your SQUACKers' perspective before the end of the SQUACK session or explicitly state that you will follow up with Questions later.

Your inquiry is likely to expose how your stakeholder thinks. Asking follow-up Questions may either improve your current deliverable or provide context for later. Each stakeholder has a different vantage point, so they may crave ways to connect your deliverable to another goal. Best of all, your Questions may prompt better ideas from the SQUACKer.

In real life

I typically review dozens of designs and other deliverables every month for various teams both in person and remotely. I strive to make Suggestions that connect our work across teams, products, experiences, and geographies.

I admit that in a spur-of-the-moment review, my Suggestions may not be perfectly thought out and may lack details.

I truly appreciate when a designer asks Questions that encourage me to weigh my thoughts, compose my intent, and balance my expectations. Although answering those Questions burns calories and possibly brain cells, I don't regret the chance to clarify my stream-of-consciousness ideas.

Don't dread upgrading a Suggestion to a Critical.

As a maker, you can upgrade a Suggestion to a Critical, especially when a customer could be negatively impacted if the issue is not resolved.

When you upgrade feedback, you are ensuring that the appropriate change is made. Stakeholders will appreciate the serious consideration you make when listening to and acting on their feedback.

In real life

Our team designed digital investment products for a full-service financial services company. When we socialized our tools outside our immediate team, the credit card team raised Questions and made Suggestions we had never considered.

The needs of credit card customers had eluded us. We definitely couldn't risk confusing our shared audience. I rephrased the team's Suggestions as Critical issues that needed to be resolved before we could launch our product. I paraphrased their concern and demonstrated that I understood the potential negative impact if we didn't take action. They celebrated that I heard them.

In response to upgrading their Suggestion to a Critical issue, my partner, Sunjay Pandey who led the product managers, said, "It shows real maturity of the UX process. That's world class and has a triple effect on diplomacy—we are willing to listen, act, and change."

Reflect on previous unresolved Suggestions.

If you do not show that you heard your stakeholder's previous Suggestion, they may boost it into a Critical issue. So, list any previous Suggestions and describe how you resolved them, how they informed your decisions, or why you ignored or downplayed them. Share your rationale and welcome more discussion if the stakeholders disagree.

By proactively describing your rationale, your stakeholders may be less likely to inflate their Suggestion into a Critical. You will need to present your argument rationally, and thoroughly explain the risk of their Suggestion in terms of cost, time, or other justification.

Be transparent about the status, before the stakeholders inquire about their cherished Suggestion.

In real life

Ima Ginary designed an experience in which a customer would request a replacement debit card online and then would receive the card at the branch office. A respected stakeholder recommended we include a few next steps on the app's confirmation screen, including the phone number needed to activate the card.

Her Suggested steps mirrored those on the pamphlet we mail to the customer with their debit card attached. Since the stakeholder already had legal approval for the text, she wanted to save us from that tedious process.

Without having the replacement card in hand, those next steps weren't applicable.

Customers didn't need to read those steps until they actually had the card (or, if they picked it up at the branch, they wouldn't need that phone number at all because the identification could be done in person with a banker).

So, Ima appropriately elected to disregard the Suggestion and then sought legal approval for the new text that described the online next steps.

Unfortunately, Ima neglected to close the loop with the stakeholder. Being ignored without any explanation, the stakeholder intensified her Suggestion into a Critical, clamoring to halt the launch of the online experience.

As a team, we repaired the relationship with this stakeholder and met our deadlines. Socializing our decisions and explaining our rationale helped avoid churn, delay, and distrust.

Translate stakeholder opinions into Suggestions.

You can clarify an opinion by paraphrasing it as an actionable Suggestion. An opinion tends to start with a phrase such as "I don't like" or "I don't think" or "Have you seen." You can offer a paraphrase, as in "It sounds like your Suggestion is to *do this … because …* ."

More candidly, let's assume your stakeholder expresses his opinion in this way: "I don't like the robotic voice you selected. We need her to sound like she wants to listen and be your friend. The robot is harsh and cold. No one is going to like her." You could paraphrase this opinion into a Suggestion in at least two ways.

1. ""Are you suggesting I slow the voice down so that it sounds friendlier?"
2. "Are you suggesting I change the words so that she sounds less formal?"

You could even paraphrase mischievously to spur a reaction: "It sounds like you're suggesting that *I* read the script because my voice is so comforting?"

Notice that each paraphrase ends with a question mark. If you raise your pitch at the end of the statement, it will sound more like an inquiry, which invites your SQUACKers to agree or at least respond to you.

But be cautious. If you end all your paraphrases or comments with an uptalk inflection, you may sound less confident.

Ideally, the squawkers recognize and copy how you have arranged the words to make a Suggestion. In doing so, they become SQUACKers and make their feedback actionable.

In real life

I've heard stakeholders complain that something needs to stand out "bigger" or "brighter." I know that if everything is big and bright on an interface, zero things end up big and zippo bright.

As tempting as it is to ignore these comments, I strive to avoid painful irritation and choose to assume positive intent. I invite stakeholders to participate in a SQUACK review, answer their Questions about SQUACK, and help them rephrase their opinions into Suggestions. I ask them to alter their complaints, likes, and opinions into Suggestion statements: "My Suggestion is to use our established design patterns. We already know they work."

Asking them to rephrase their opinion into a Suggestion encourages them to focus on the action they intend the designer to take. When stakeholders want something to *pop* more, they may believe having more people start the process will result in more people finishing the process. I focus instead on the need to have more of those people who start the process actually finish it, instead of assuming that if we have more people starting, we'll have more people finishing. Our goals are the same, but we have different assumptions and action items.

I also make sure people feel heard, by repeating the phrase that seems most important. That echoing encourages people to expand their thoughts, possibly revealing their true need. So, by reiterating, "Make it pop?" you may encourage the stakeholders to dive deeper and describe what action is needed.

It's a choice.

I imagine they think they are actually helping with such opinions. I proactively envision working together to translate their "make it pop" into a change we'd enthusiastically consider. When I assume positive intent, I can ask Questions to understand why they need something a certain way and identify ways to measure our shared success.

Q FOR QUESTIONS

Definition: An area that needs clarity or exploration.

Formula:

$$\left\{ \begin{array}{c} \text{type of Question} \\ = \\ \text{type of answer} \\ \text{nothing } + \text{ or } - \end{array} \right\}$$

Color: Orange signifies exploration and harmony. So orange represents Questions to encourage you to dive deep and investigate.

Symbol: ? The question mark is increasingly being added to international keyboards. It is on track to become a universal symbol.

Remember the formula for Questions.

Contemplate the type of Questions you are being asked. Does the stakeholder want a "yes" or "no" response so that she can follow up with more questions? Or is she asking for more details from you?

Some stakeholders may only ask questions they can answer, whereas other stakeholders may ask questions to expand their knowledge. Remember that you are the expert; your stakeholders didn't create your deliverable. Until you understand your stakeholders' goal, you should only answer the type of Question you're being asked. Listen to the tone and style of their Questions. Sometimes they will rapid-fire a follow-up Question that uncovers their focus. To understand their intent, ask them clarifying Questions too.

If your initial answer doesn't match the Question type, your stakeholder may lose confidence in you and, by extension, your work. This sounds drastic, but think about this classic example: if your stakeholder eagerly asks, "What time is it?" she does not need to know what type of watch you're wearing and how accurate it is. And if she doesn't know whether she's running late, the extra information would only infuriate her.

Understanding the Question coupled with your stakeholders' intent helps you, in turn, be less evasive and more precise in how you answer their Questions.

In real life

When someone on the project team fails to answer the specific Question I asked, I have several possible reactions.

As a UX manager or stakeholder, I may become skeptical of their deliverable, which causes me to dig deeper to expose the weakness.

I may become offended because they are not listening or asking clarifying questions.

I may recognize that my Question, position, or approach may have been intimidating.

These are not constructive reactions.

Instead, makers need to pay attention to the Question and answer it. If they don't have an answer, I would prefer they paraphrase the Question to show they understand what I am asking, declare that they don't have an answer now, and then tell me when they will get back to me with the answer.

Don't feel obligated to answer Questions in advance.

One of the biggest mistakes when reviewing your deliverable is trying to proactively answer every potential Question you could get. Yes, I know. This principle seems to contradict the others, especially the recommendation to provide sufficient context about your work.

It doesn't.

You should anticipate Questions and at least mentally answer them. Overcome that undying compulsion to actually answer every possible inquiry before you're even asked. Just thinking through the answers will build your confidence for when those Questions do arise.

I am not advising you to hide information or WARTS from your stakeholders. Your job includes showing confidence in your work. When you have made the right decisions under whatever constraints you face, you owe your stakeholders a demonstration of that confidence.

When you know something could be better, you owe your stakeholders that context. If you have solved a problem your stakeholders no longer have to worry about, you no longer need to describe those details.

Determine how to answer your stakeholders' Questions so that they understand how to help you move forward, but don't feel obligated to share every detail until and unless you are asked.

In real life

Let's consider an anti-example from a Fortune 200 company. We had 300+ stakeholders lining the walls in the executive conference center awaiting the results of a recent survey. The researcher began with 45 slides about the method, participants, tasks, script, questions, timeline, calculations—the answers to every trivial background question he could imagine.

The response? Napping. Snoring. Leaving.

Stakeholders ignored the results because they never heard them. They just wanted to assume the researcher had done his due diligence, learn about the key insights, and evaluate the recommended action items.

So, simplify stakeholders' decisions by minimizing the "noise" about your scientific method, your tradeoffs, and the obstacles you overcame. Force yourself to describe your research method in two sentences and reference the details in your appendix. Reveal what your stakeholders need to hear and the actions they need to take—not the hardships you endured when planning, collecting, and analyzing the results.

Consider whether the Question is intended for you or a peer.

High performers may pledge to answer every Question. I Kudo their bias for action and Suggest that they consider who needs or even deserves to answer each Question.

You may indeed have an appropriate and reasonable answer, but others could have more expertise or more context to share with the group. So, let them answer Questions that pertain to their discipline so that you can highlight your expertise, too.

Honor others with the chance to explain or even boast.

In real life

As a UX leader, I typically manage the design, research, and content disciplines. When reviewing a design, I may ask about the intent behind an interaction that I am SQUACKing. I may not be asking about the design rationale. I might actually want to hear the product manager describe what the user or the product is intended to accomplish. If I ask this Question early in the product life cycle, it's likely an indicator that I suspect the product intent is not clear.

The discipline responsible for providing that clarity is product, not UX.

The UX team may start to answer the Question based on how they understand the intent. But I may virtually elbow them to be quiet. I want to hear from the product folks to see how well they can explain the intent. If they are concise, I have more confidence that UX team can succeed. If the intent is not clear, I keep prompting for information to arm the team with the insights they need.

Timelines and scope are another concern intended for the product team, while platform and scalability are intended for the tech discipline. It's important that each discipline takes accountability for the areas it drives. When a designer answers Questions about technical microservices, I worry that we're accepting responsibility for elements that need to be owned by others.

Uncover the root cause of a constraining Question.

Developers are creative problem solvers. Analysis and design are typically the first steps in both the development process and in our design UX process. They're different concepts for each discipline but they overlap in intent.

So, our developers need to ask clarifying Questions. Unfortunately, we may overinterpret their Questions as an imperative that we must solve. The implication seems to be that we need to change the design to conform more conveniently to the code. Their Questions should not be intended to throw a design with positive User Signal back to us for undesirable changes.

The developer must explore options and uncover obstacles, and may even, subtly, be evaluating our conviction about a particular interaction.

Sometimes Questions test our conviction—if we bend the design to simplify the development work, we imply a lack of confidence. Rather than responding immediately to a developer's request or an unrecognized constraint, I recommend delaying your answer and absolutely avoiding the phrases "I think" and "I feel." In fact, we should shun the word *I* when answering Questions to avoid implying that our decisions are subjective, rather than user- or expertise-driven.

I am happy to negotiate tradeoffs. But first, I reframe their Question to understand the actual constraint: "You seem worried about needing a new component with this design. Is the novelty your primary concern?" Notice that I phrase my "why" Question with "seem" to diminish the intensive tone. My clarifying Question engages and explores our shared options. Then our solution (informed via both UX analysis + design steps and the corresponding developer analysis + design steps) is more comprehensive and less jeopardizing to both the user experience and the quality of the code.

We may also discover, together, that their original Question no longer applies. Seriously.

In real life

When our team created a new interaction for our mobile app, I anticipated many Questions from our development team as they dissected the headache ahead for them to code it for both Android and iOS devices.

I feared our design team would misinterpret the technical Questions as reluctance or doubt. I didn't want the UXers to accept Questions as a request to update our design. We needed to be patient.

Afterall, I'm a big believer in the eureka moment that designers experience in the middle of the night. In fact, my nightstand contains a Moleskine, a fountain pen, and a headlamp so I can sketch the random midnight solutions to the previous day's insufferable challenges.

Why can't developers experience that same midnight revelation? They can and do, especially when they have enough time to contemplate and juggle ideas.

I noticed a playful spark in the developer's eye on Monday. After musing about the challenge our design posed to her technical code, she joined our stand-up meeting bright and early with a striking solution. No painful design tradeoffs were even required.

I've seen this innovative fire multiple times. I'm bummed when we, in UX, thwart the developers from solving a problem because we've accepted their implied tradeoff request too quickly. When we assume the constraint, then we—not they—get to solve the problem.

Note:

I do not endorse surprising our tech partners. Their creative problem-solving can expand our options if we involve them in iteration and research activities as early as possible.

That problem may not even apply if we just practice a little patience. Let's not rush our development partners through their analysis and design steps.

And if our deadlines prevent the developers enough time to explore and dream, ask them Questions to expose why our design is challenging to code. The root cause of the challenge can reveal different, some non-design oriented, solutions.

My favorite exploratory Question is "If we don't adopt that change, how would you solve for it?" The implication is that I do not want to change but I do want to understand the situation.

Some root causes may need human interaction (training or improving skills), while others may require super-hero powers to overcome (mind control may be needed to mitigate regulatory requirements or time travel may be required to enable platform-level capabilities).

So, avoid thinking that their initial Questions are change requests and don't adjust your design until the developers have had time to consider the challenge and you understand the true constraint.

What if you don't have an answer to a Question?

First, Kudo the stakeholder for asking an insightful Question. Then determine whether you should have the answer. If you should but don't, let the stakeholder know when you will follow up. If you need help getting the answer, ask the stakeholder for advice, guidance, or clarity. Your SQUACKers can then volunteer more information or may rephrase the Question for better clarity.

Lastly, let folks know when you will follow up. And then, ahem, follow up.

In real life

An executive stakeholder once asked me why my deliverable didn't consider the data from one of the company's dashboards. I couldn't actually answer this "why" Question without revealing my manager's failure to share the information with me. "Why" questions tend to put people on the defensive as they attempt to explain or justify themselves.

I had no idea what data or dashboard he meant.

Instead of outing my manager, I skirted with a follow-up query. "What data do you think is most relevant?" He responded with a precise scenario. To which I said I hadn't considered that point of view and wondered if he could interpret the data for me so that I had more details to consider.

He agreed to set up a future meeting, my boss saved face, and I had access to that data going forward.

What if you're not sure you know the answer to a Question?

First, clarify the Question. Paraphrasing demonstrates that you understand the SQUACKer's intent. Then you have a couple of options.

You can say, "Here's what I *do* know" and describe related information. By emphasizing the word "do," you're admitting that you may not be answering the actual Question. You're begging for a little forgiveness and opening the door for further clarification. This option works especially well when you have related concerns, constraints, or constructive elements that haven't been raised yet. It doesn't work well if you're merely repeating known information.

Your other option is to say you will need to get back with the answer. You'll earn more positive impressions if you specify a deadline for providing the answer. It's important to show you understand the Question so that the stakeholders trust you will pursue the needed information and will follow up.

You may also discover the stakeholders may not expect an actual answer. They may admit they are spurring you to think more deeply or differently.

In real life

Early in my career, I was asked a divisive Question and I wasn't sure I could answer it, especially in front of several team members. Flustered, I declared that I would respond offline. I constructed my response later that day.

Actually, I immediately wrote my response.

Doubted it.

Rewrote it.

Escaped to the walking trail behind the building to contemplate.

Returned to my desk.

Hit the *Send* button.

Within 10 minutes, the general manager stepped into my office. I was steeped in my work. His appearance startled me.

He impatiently interrupted and obviously was a bit irritated. He rephrased his Question after seeing my lengthy response. I answered immediately.

He smiled and left.

Naturally, I was immersed in the details. I'd answered honestly, only to discover that I had interpreted his Question erroneously and provided the wrong details. Stakeholders typically need a peripheral understanding of the overarching concept, not all the implementation details.

The next time, I asked him to clarify his Questions before leaving the meeting.

Determine when to answer each Question—now or later?

If your answer to a stakeholder's Question requires a backstory, consider answering later via a message, discussion, or document. Your SQUACKer may insist on hearing an answer; but if you demonstrate that you understand her Question, you likely can delay until you have a succinct and clear response.

If, over time, you recognize that your stakeholders repeatedly veer away from the original discussion, consider whether your previous answers have introduced new or disconcerting topics. Your wandering answers may entice your stakeholders to meander through irrelevant details.

You may want to visibly capture their Questions (on a whiteboard or in a shared document) so that they know they've been heard. Then, respond to them offline, after you've had a chance to write concise answers.

In real life

Em Bellisher loved sharing anecdotes about her design process with charm, wit, and energy. She was confident in her approach and how she tied all the details together. Her storytelling style was appreciated during the pitch—when we are garnering financial investments and resources for the concept. Later, after we've committed to a deadline or set expectations with stakeholders, her colorful candor can be misleading and cause lots of unnecessary churn.

We leverage Em's natural ability to envision the impossible early in the life cycle, and transition to a fact-based presentation rather than visionary storytelling later in the life cycle. That way, we don't needlessly alarm our stakeholders when they are most stressed about the actual delivery of the product.

Transitioning from envisioning to fact was an exacting science at Microsoft. Once we publicly announced the general availability date for software or cloud service, no leader wanted to punt on that promise to our customers. As that date loomed, stakeholders only wanted facts. No envisioning, no embellishing, no new risks.

Remember, silence is golden.

Be comfortable with silence before and after you answer a Question. Silence can feel awkward, but that silence may allow you to compose a better answer and your stakeholders to articulate a clearer follow-up Question.

You can stall quietly while you think of an answer or contemplate ways to reframe the Question.

Take the time you need to formulate an answer. Worst case? Offer to respond after the SQUACK session.

In real life

I typically write the Question on a whiteboard, slowly and artistically to stall for time. It's a cue: if my handwriting is legible, I'm triggering my brain to think intensely. It's a delay tactic.

I may buy more time by cracking a joke or shooting a playfully glaring look at the stakeholder who dared to ask such a profound Question. I may simply paraphrase the Question back while I gather my thoughts and articulate an answer.

Once, I wrote the Question on the whiteboard, grabbed the red marker, and drew a star. I told the group: "I promise I'll answer, but I need time to think." I then asked someone to give me a 5-minute warning before the end of the meeting—forcing me to answer that stellar Question before we left.

All of this posturing lets me postpone and sort things through mentally. Although I fill the silence with an entertaining distraction, you're not obligated to do that. Take the time you need, and if you suspect the SQUACKers are growing impatient, paraphrase the Question to ensure that you understand it and then let them know when you plan to answer.

Delay answering Questions that could reignite previous debates

Controversy typically happens when the ideal experience conflicts with or challenges the business policies or technical constraints. As a team, you may have acquiesced to a less-than-ideal solution for the design, business, or technology disciplines.

You may finally feel relieved that a decision has been made. You may even feel prepared to advocate for the less-than-ideal decision after debating with your team.

Unfortunately, stakeholder Questions may unintentionally reignite a debate that caused you to gnash your teeth or lose sleep.

If you feel like the decision jeopardized your discipline or your expertise, you especially need to be silent. If the Question feels awkward to answer because you will have to take the counterargument, let the person who supports that side of the debate answer the Question. If you've worked through the debate and lost, wait for the person you disagreed with to answer, particularly if the stakeholder who asked the Question represents that person's discipline. The person who answers the Question essentially must defend the controversial conclusion. Do not answer dispassionately.

Instead, delay.

Let other disciplines answer these Questions.

The stakeholders may in fact be leaning toward your side of the argument. When you speak up defending the "other" side, the stakeholders will likely assume you agree. They won't bother to ask whether you are advocating wholeheartedly or passively.

In real life

Our team finally agreed on the scope of our MVP (minimally viable product) release. But no one was happy.

Em Bellisher, a senior designer and gifted storyteller, felt strongly that the first release provided only minimal experimentation value and no user delight. Nonetheless, the team had worked through numerous constraints, concerns, and conflicts. They accepted the WARTS.

Em hosted a SQUACK review with managers who advocated for users as well as for goals that conflicted with our design goals. The team set context with unabashed transparency about the constraints and tradeoffs they faced. They had determinedly emerged from the conflict and landed on a tolerable solution. They had one another's backs because they understood all sides of the argument.

An executive stakeholder asked multiple Questions about the timelines, constraints, and design tradeoffs. I suspected that Em felt obligated to answer each Question, since the UX team initiated the SQUACK review.

I knew she hardly applauded the tradeoff decisions and dreaded advocating for the resulting design.

Working remotely, I texted her: "Breathe, Em, be patient."

If we had been in the same room, I would have cued her with a cough (or playfully an elbow). She needed to let the product owner, who worked directly for the stakeholder asking the Questions, to lead the discussion.

After listening, the stakeholder directed her next Question to the designer. "Em, is this the right design?"

Em responded that, given the constraints the team faced, this was the right design. Her loyalty to the team remained intact. She held the line with the tradeoffs the team had established.

The discussion then moved to the leadership team. We discussed whether we agreed with the tradeoffs and debated levers we could use to alleviate the original constraints. Ultimately, the business stakeholder released the product person from a constrictive requirement. The tension eased. The team then described improvements they could make with the reframed constraints.

After the session, I debriefed with Em. She considered how, if I hadn't urged her patience, she would have artificially answered the Questions. She could have projected a false sense of confidence in the resulting design.

We discussed how to spot an open door that just needed the right decision maker to walk through and update our constraints.

U FOR USER SIGNAL

Definition: Data, feedback, or research that spurs a compelling Suggestion or authentic Kudos.

Formula:

$$\left\{ \begin{array}{c} \text{describe known User Signal} \\ + \\ \text{if veering, share Suggestion to improve} \\ \text{or} \\ \text{if aligning, describe expected Kudos} \end{array} \right\}$$

Color: Purple is the color of royalty in Victorian paintings. So, purple represents User Signal to show a similar sense of importance.

Symbol: • • • An ellipsis reminds us that we need to fill in blanks from what the users said or did. We either form strong Suggestions, backed by user evidence, or significant Kudos, informed by users first hand.

Help stakeholders unpack User Signal to reveal either Suggestions or Kudos.

When teams implement the SQUACK feedback formula, they tend to ponder more about User Signal than any other category. User Signal is a transitional category that originates with users and then morphs into either strong Suggestions or impactful Kudos. User Signal requires you to research, listen, observe, or analyze your users to amplify Suggestions or Kudos.

Frankly, if user research routinely strengthens the design concepts, improves the work in progress (low-fidelity wireframes or high-fidelity prototypes), or informs the success of the launched product, there's zero reason to brag. And there's no reason to mention User Signal.

If the design veers from known User Signal, the resulting Suggestion may involve collecting more user data, validating the decision before

A note for grammar gurus: Professional user researchers know the danger of acting on a single data point—one person's opinion, observation, or action does not represent the overall audience. When I mention User Signal, I assume the research is both valid (you collected the data authentically and without bias) and reliable (if you repeated the study, you'd collect similar results). As a category within the SQUACK formula, User Signal is a singular noun. But within the text, User Signal refers to a collection of valid and reliable research, so I treat it as a plural collective noun. Phew. Complicated.

launching, throttling the launch to a small number of users initially, or mitigating the risk another way.

For example, let's say your User Signal indicates that customers want to solve problems for themselves, without having to call for help. A subsequent Suggestion might be to highlight the searchable help first, rather than emphasizing the phone number, which may imply that you expect users to encounter problems. Then, after their first query, you show your phone number. You can collect data to determine whether the query actually resolved their problem and enabled them to be successful without help. This Suggestion relies on the known User Signal to make a recommendation.

Likewise, if the deliverable elegantly solves customer problems, simplifies their lives, or provides a moment of delight, you can mention the existing User Signal and end with a heartfelt, data-informed Kudo. For example, let's say your User Signal indicates customers are confused about the difference between paying their friend via a person-to-person platform versus through a bill pay service. The Kudos may show appreciation for providing descriptions based on real-life use cases for both options in a conversational tone: "You created a proactive solution that required minimal coding but will relieve major user confusion."

Amplify User Signal by encouraging your stakeholders to participate.

After you conduct user research, you likely can describe how users think about your concept, how they reacted to your designs, and what iterations will be needed after making tradeoff decisions to get the product launched. You want your stakeholders to be informed and participate in understanding users too.

You also want your stakeholders to empathize with users. When you have successfully shared user research, your stakeholders volunteer User Signal based on first-hand knowledge. They are proud to express how the deliverable meets those needs and they Kudo you for that alignment.

If you haven't included your stakeholders in your user research, they may not know how to use the User Signal category. Ideally, they can quote your user research results back to you as Suggestions when you've veered from the signal and as Kudos when you've aligned to or even exceeded your users' expectations.

In real life

The UX team I managed at Microsoft invited our stake-holders from the marketing, business, and technical disciplines to join our on-site visits with customers. Our group program manager, Ford McKinstry, observed that not all companies have dedicated IT departments. "They have to do all their own tech support. I had no idea that normal, non-tech people (like Greg, one of the customers we visited) had to troubleshoot their systems at work."

He expressed his growing empathy for technology avoiders. During one design review, he said, "Let's make sure to solve Greg's problem for him—he shouldn't have to think about the domain name server to get his email." When we reviewed the final design, Ford exclaimed, "I wish I could see Greg's face when he gets this. We just stopped a major headache for him."

Years later, that comment remains one of my favorite Kudos for a system that solved real user problems. This Kudo is more significant than if Ford had simply said "Great job solving user pain points," because authentic User Signal led to that unforgettable Kudo.

Let your users talk for you.

Ideally, your research participants, who match your target audience, can describe how well your design meets their needs. You can observe their reactions to the design and capture their thoughts as they think aloud. The recordings of real people during a usability test, site visits, interviews, or focus groups can be convincing, especially if you did not have to prompt your users to say positive or negative things.

In real life

I've adapted psychology professor Robert Plutchik's Wheel of Emotions to encourage research participants to express what they are feeling. Dr. Plutchik established the wheel to help people identify the intersections of emotions. In a usability test or other research study, the emotional intersection is not important. My intent is to provide a vocabulary for usability participants to react to, rather than responding to an open-ended question.

The version I use is a table, because it's easier to read a table on a screen than it is to twist your head around Dr. Plutchik's wheel. My emotion table is (intentionally) neither scientific nor comprehensive. It's a mechanism to encourage average people who agree to participate in a study to open up and discuss their feelings.

I've used the emotion table mostly in the financial services industry. We display the table and ask the participants to think about their current financial situation. We ask them to select three feelings from the list and then describe why they feel that way.

Then we invite the participants to complete the usability tasks. At the end of the session, we remind them about the three words they used. We ask them if and how their feelings have changed after using our design.

The words they select are less important than their descriptions about why they feel the way they do. The emotion table provides a framework to unlock those thoughts and helps people express themselves.

How has it worked? When our team created a tool to provide digital financial advice, a young customer said she selected "abandoned" because she was "completely alone" in making financial decisions. "I have no idea if I'm doing things right, and my husband just doesn't want to deal with the money," she said, adding, "I feel so deserted."

As stakeholders and makers, we didn't want to hear despair. No one wants to hear misery.

Hearing the emotional comments from our users motivated us—to change people's lives, to improve their finances, to take action.

With the emotion table you'll learn more about *why* someone feels the way they do than you would if you just asked them to numerically rate how satisfied they were with the design. The emotion table I have used appears on the following page. You may want to list emotions that match your brand or design principles.

Happy	Sad	Disgusted
Accepted	Abandoned	Awful
Amused	Apathetic	Detested
Confident	Ashamed	Disappointed
Courageous	Bored	Disapproved
Ecstatic	Despair	Discouraged
Fulfilled	Embarrassed	Dreadful
Hopeful	Empty	Hesitant
Important	Guilty	Horrible
Inquisitive	Ignored	Judged
Inspired	Inferior	Loathed
Interested	Isolated	Nauseating
Joyful	Lonely	Offended
Loved	Lost	Ostracized
Optimistic	Miserable	Repugnant
Peaceful	Powerless	Shunned
Powerful	Victimized	Sick
Proud	Vulnerable	Terrible

Angry	Fearful	Surprised
Aggressive	Alienated	Amazed
Antagonistic	Anxious	Ambitious
Critical	Disrespected	Astonished
Detached	Frightened	Awed
Frustrated	Humiliated	Confused
Hateful	Inadequate	Disillusioned
Hopeless	Inferior	Dismayed
Hostile	Insecure	Eager
Hurt	Insignificant	Energetic
Infuriated	Nervous	Enthusiastic
Mad	Overwhelmed	Excited
Provoked	Rejected	Motivated
Sarcastic	Ridiculed	Passionate
Skeptical	Scared	Perplexed
Suspicious	Submissive	Puzzled
Threatened	Worried	Shocked
Withdrawn	Worthless	Startled

Determine if/when collecting additional User Signal is merited.

Usability and research can become a crutch if you try to verify every design decision with user input. How demoralizing it would be if every decision needed to be validated. Of course, if a decision is risky (in terms of lost revenue, increasing costs, lost loyalty, or poor reviews), you may decide to collect validating User Signal. You may want to launch the design, if possible, to a small audience first, measure the reaction, and if things go well, increase the release to a larger audience until you reach all your users.

Decide what your target measures are in advance. Once you meet those targets, your decision to launch the design will be clearly data informed.

In real life

While I was a graduate student, I helped redesign the city of Bloomington's website for class. We interviewed citizens to understand their needs, observed the switchboard operators to understand why people called the city, interviewed stakeholders to understand what they expected from the website, and conducted usability tests to identify and then mitigate problems with the existing site. After following this user-centered design process, we had confidence in our redesign.

But we made a fatal mistake.

We failed to set any target measures with the stakeholders.

We released the design to 30% of the website's visitors. We noted that searching for "swimming pool hours" resulted in the Parks and Recreation page. So, as graduate students, we felt confident that those citizens successfully located the information they needed.

But we didn't know if relying on the search functionality meant the new design succeeded or failed.

We should have set a target that if at least 70% of searches had successful queries, the city could confidently launch the redesign. As far as I know, the redesign never launched, because no one could say whether it met the success criteria or not. I'm glad I learned that lesson during school and not on the job.

Solve hopeless user problems with grit and data.

What happens if your organization claims it can't solve a user pain point because doing so contradicts the business model or bruises the ego of an important stakeholder? Don't fret. Diligently collect proof that the user problem exists.

If you neglect to collect and report the data, the change may never occur. Patience and diligence are vital.

Converting anecdotal complaints, which are easy to ignore, into an actual number of complaints results in tangible evidence. If it takes months or years, be calm and collect more data. Track and publicize the frequency of the problem. Once you have sufficient evidence, the doubt about solving the impossible problem will likely diminish. No more anecdotes. Instead, you can ask, "How can we afford *not* to fix this problem that X number of our customers experienced?"

In real life

At USAA, our early website navigation mirrored our organizational structure. We had links for auto, home, and life insurance, as well as links for investments, banking, and the business area that provided discounts and rewards for rental cars, flowers, jewelry, and other luxury items. The name of the company, Alliance Services Company (ASC), did not innately reflect the products it offered. The link, out of respect for (or really at the demand of) the company president, was predictably "Alliance Services Company".

ASC's president epitomized an Egoma Niac stakeholder. She had metaphorically bloodied the career ladder as she earned her spot at the top. Blatantly proud of her position, she fought hard to be assessed as equal to the other presidents within the corporate structure. She commanded a line-of-business within a Fortune 200 company. Without a doubt, an enormous accomplishment.

Our design team, based on the User Signal we had collected, wanted her to change the name of the company (really, just the link name). Unfortunately, that request bruised her ego. So, we continued to collect User Signal via video clips from usability tests.

When I've shared this story, UX people are aghast that we were unable to fix such an obvious problem that could've been resolved with a mere label change. Sadly, we sometimes forget that people, who are flawed, egotistical, and self-absorbed, make decisions.

Tenacity overcame the executive's weaknesses. Our research team stubbornly piggybacked a shopping task on every test, no matter what the actual study covered:

- "How would you locate cruise tickets?"
- "Where would you go to find discounts for rental cars?" and
- "Where would you purchase an engagement ring?"

Usability participants said they would have to call for help; none of the links looked correct. They never once said they would select the "Alliance Services Company" link. When we probed further and asked, "What would you expect if you clicked that link?" their answers varied. None was correct.

Several executives warned me to avoid conversing about link names with the ASC president. Especially if I valued my career. Despite the warnings, I knew we had enough evidence that I could at least confidentially discuss this usability problem with her. Our video lowlight reel showed confused members struggling to find the products and services she'd diligently built and managed.

I shared ideas for changing the link, based on User Signal, and she made the final choice: member discounts. We didn't see the usability problem again, and the digital metrics for ASC immediately improved.

The president also became an advocate for User Signal.

A FOR ACCIDENT

Definition: A typo, copy / paste error, misalignment, or math mistake.

Formula:

$$\left\{ \begin{array}{c} \text{<discretion>} \\ \qquad \text{highlight the } \mathbf{A}\text{ccident} \\ + \\ \wedge \text{ tell the feedback recipient} \\ \textit{privately} \qquad\qquad \text{</discretion>} \end{array} \right\}$$

Color: Accidents are green because careless errors are natural. We should feel lucky, as in a green four-leaf clover, that we identified the Accidents before our users saw them.

Symbol: ⋀ The caret is a copyediting symbol meaning to insert a letter, word, or phrase, or to collapse spaces or paragraphs.

Share the formula for Accidents.

Remind your stakeholders that they do not need to call out Accidents during the SQUACK review. Instead, they can circle the mistake, mark it with an *A*, provide the correction (if needed), and either give the paper copy back to you at the end of the meeting or just post it in the meeting chat.

Stakeholders likely will appreciate ignoring inconsequential errors that you can easily fix and instead focus their time on providing more strategic and impactful feedback.

The errors still get fixed, but you don't have to discuss them as a team.

For example

eet
^
The thoughtful manager discretely marked the typo.

Don't irritate accountants with mathematical errors.

Understand what is important to your stakeholders and triple-check your work. For example, accountants are primed to notice calculation errors. If you make up numbers for demonstration or placement only, your stakeholders may still mentally calculate your accuracy. All numbers feel real to mathematicians, regardless of how much you strive to convince them your calculations are pretend, for example only, or just hard-coded onto a prototype (not actually calculated).

When your accountant stakeholders notice an Accident, they will scrutinize everything more meticulously. They'll posit that if you can make a math error (shock!), what else are you capable of doing? How careless are you?

So, if your stakeholders are accountants, make sure any calculations, numbers, or algorithms you use are logical, realistic, and accurate, even on low-fidelity designs.

In real life

When our team designed a tool to calculate volume-licensing discounts at Microsoft, we created a mockup of the bill with example discounts, training rewards, terms, conditions, residuals, and costs. The fictitious numbers in our example applied to medium-size organizations with enterprise agreements. When we presented the design to our accounting stakeholder, we spent 45 precious minutes watching him do mental gymnastics to refute our math. We told him emphatically, loudly, repeatedly:

"The calculation is just an example."

"These numbers are for placement only."

"Don't worry! Customers will never see this!"

Nothing stopped him from calculating. He simply couldn't imagine being inaccurate, intentionally or inadvertently. Something had to be wrong with us, our approach, and our results.

True.

We had failed. Our meaningless minutiae troubled an accountant's expertise. Our placeholder text proved to be no shortcut, because we unintentionally insulted him and his profession.

Avoid irritating the grammarians.

If your stakeholders are linguists or logophiles, they will likely anguish over a grammatical error in your deliverable, which, in turn, will erode their trust and intensify their scrutiny of your work.

If you use Latin placeholder text, a grammarian guru may try to convince you that the syntax is incorrect.

So, take the time to add real content to your low-fidelity designs and triple-check your spelling, grammar, style, and tone.

In real life

When we moved to Seattle, my husband and I committed to the change:

- Selling our first home, a 1927 cottage we refurbished to become part of the historical neighborhood's show of homes
- Moving 2,000 miles from Texas sunshine to Washington rain
- Buying a home four times more expensive than the one we left
- Adding 12 inches to the largest travel kennel so that our giant malamute could safely stretch and turn around on the flight
- Watching my husband hobble on crutches after double knee-replacement surgery and still getting the house packed

I committed to my new job. My home, my husband, my dogs were all in. Deep.

I waited and waded through weeks of mind-numbing feedback, initially about grammar. My manager wanted complete sentences for each item in the table of contents for the UX strategy document.

Then he wanted verb-leading phrases.

The next week, bullet points.

Followed by numbers.

Then Roman numerals.

He pondered whether periods, dashes, or spaces should separate the title from the page number.

He debated about ALL CAPs versus Title Case.

He argued whether *A*, *An*, and *The* should be capitalized.

I couldn't quit, despite my frustration. I had to work through the torment. I finally changed tactics. I eliminated the entire table of contents. I told the story from midpoint forward and then backed up to review the overarching structure.

All in one meeting.

No angst. No debate. No torment.

I stopped irritating the grammarian. If SQUACK had existed, I would have sent him the document in advance and asked him to discreetly identify any Accidents. SQUACK could have avoided all the wasted hours.

Prevent perplexing the pixel perfectionists.

Maybe your stakeholder gets migraines due to inconsistent color hues or has pixel-perfect eyes that ache when graphic elements are misaligned. If you are not so pixel inclined, you may want to SQUACK with this stakeholder interactively—so that you can make the changes instantly.

Fixing mathematical, grammatical, and pixel Accidents should be easy—perhaps time consuming, but easy because there's an obvious fix.

No debate is needed before acting.

If you can prevent debates about Accidents, everyone will cheer.

In real life

I swear several of my design colleagues can distinguish misalignments, discolorations, and jarring animations 90 yards away from the screen. I need an electron microscope, a decoder ring, and a lot of luck to decipher those visual Accidents.

Unfortunately, I'm not alone.

The development team at Microsoft felt defeated and angry when they opened their bug tracking tool to discover 90 new defects filed by one of our designers. The developers wanted to dismiss the importance of matching their code to our design redlines. I had to admit that I couldn't readily detect the defects either. But, I appreciated that they existed and wanted them fixed, not ignored.

Rather than close the bugs with a status of 'by design' or 'won't fix,' I worked with the dev manager to mitigate the current issues and prevent a repeat of unexpected fit-and-finish bugs in the future releases. Our solution: reserve time for co-design once the code is stable. The front-end coders sit side-by-side with the designers and they fix the fit-and-finish issues together. No bugs are filed and problems are fixed immediately.

I strive to hire at least one designer with that visual acuity superpower to see and fix the Accidents I can't.

Take a red pen to your own Accidents. Own up to them.

When you intentionally make one or more Accidents, you need to subtly mention them. When you unintentionally make an error and you only notice it when others are reviewing your work, you need to decide whether or not to declare it out loud.

Do your stakeholders earnestly want to contribute to your success? Then consider allowing them to identify it for you, rather than pointing it out yourself.

Do your stakeholders strive to add depth to your success and enjoy challenging you to think deeper or broader, overlooking simple careless mistakes? Then discreetly capture your own simple mistake and carry on.

Do your stakeholders feel obligated to provide feedback? Then ignore your mistake and let them cherish finding it for you.

In real life

At Los Alamos National Laboratory, I waited for the printer to spit out the proposal our team of chemists had written. I needed to grab the print and quickly make 30 copies for the 9 a.m. meeting with our visiting dignitaries from Sandia National Laboratories and Lawrence Livermore National Laboratory. Our proposal would treat and manage the nation's nuclear waste materials.

For the first time, our technologies would not compete with the other laboratories. We created a joint proposal.

I pushed my luck. The printer stubbornly printed each character, word, and paragraph. A cruel master of torture.

To my horror, I had printed the wrong version.

I was young and embarrassed.

I didn't have time to run back upstairs, find the right version, and print it again.

Instead, I wrote the corrections using several copy-editing symbols on the copy that did successfully print. I wanted to indicate I knew about the careless errors. I wanted to reassure everyone I would fix the errors before we submitted our proposal to the funding agencies.

I distributed the document with the editing marks and invited the scientists to read through the proposal. No one said a word about the cryptic editing symbols.

My general manager approached me after the meeting. He congratulated me for lowering the stress in the room. My mistakes and hand-written corrections made the dignitaries, whose doctorates numbered in the dozens, consider the document as a work in progress that they could still improve. The discussion proceeded with less formality, which built stronger consensus. And he said that because no one seemed to understand my copyediting symbols, the scientists felt they could ask about each other's expertise too.

They all recognized they did not understand everything.

The hand-scrawled symbols lowered the threshold for asking Questions.

Proudly endorse all the options you present.

Jeff Atwood, who blogs "Coding Horror: programming and human factors," describes an ugly duckling as a "feature added for no other reason than to draw management attention and be removed, thus avoiding unnecessary changes in other aspects of the product."

It's an intriguing, controversial idea that may have merit, if you ensure that the duckling is redeemable and not irreversibly ugly. I first learned about the "insert an ugly duckling" advice in Tom Greever's book, Articulating Design Decisions.

Jeff's story describes a designer who drew animations for the game Battle Chess.

The designer knew his stakeholder felt obligated to provide feedback about every design.

So, he artfully animated the Queen character and added a superfluous pet duck.

He deftly planned ahead.

His flapping duck, visible throughout all the Queen's appearances, never intersected with the "actual" animation.

Eventually, after watching all the animations, the stakeholder told the artist, "That looks great. Just one thing: get rid of the duck." To meet his stakeholder's request, the designer simply eliminated the duck with a few lines of code.

Voilà!

The stakeholder claims a win, the designer does not feel like a pawn, and no checkmate is required.

This advice met the stakeholder's need to contribute to the designer's success.

My advice:

Don't tempt your luck.

Your stakeholder may adore that duck.

And then your design will be stuck.

In real life

Although I've never included an ugly duckling in my work, I did create a placeholder design that I later deeply regretted.

As the web team for Indiana University, we wanted to showcase the breadth and variation of the university ecosystem because each campus embodied a different vibe.

Have you heard about Indiana University, the party school? That means the Bloomington campus.

Professional offerings for mature students? IUPUI in Indianapolis.

Extensive medical degree programs? The Fort Wayne campus.

Small class sizes with personal attention? That could be the campus in Columbus, Kokomo, or Richmond.

Each campus harnessed a unique offering that deserved a spotlight on the integrated university website. I spearheaded the user research efforts to create that one integrated view rather than the glut of sites the university painstakingly maintained.

Part of our initial design concept used a simple crimson flag as a link for each campus.

The low-fidelity prototype proved successful in our usability tests. Although we did not measure desirability or delight, the participants could successfully apply to the campus of their choice, register for classes, and make donations. Our new navigation worked.

We anticipated skepticism from our stakeholders about the cohesive brand and site we created.

So, we prepared an in-depth discussion of our research results from across the state. We intended to show our stakeholders how effective the integrated site was.

We needed their buy-in to continue with the integration.

To my dismay, the stakeholders loved the design.

Those ugly crimson flags stuck.

I couldn't protest. I had presented that design concept proudly.

It met the stakeholders' expectations.

They approved it.

For years the Indiana.edu site boasted the design that I deemed dreadful.

I learned that as a designer, you must endorse all the designs you present to your stakeholders.

All your designs must meet your quality bar.

You cannot trust that your decision makers will notice drab or subpar work.

C FOR CRITICAL

Definition: A problem that must be resolved because of the potential business risk or customer pain.

Formula:

$$\left\{ \begin{array}{c} \text{do this} \\ + \\ \text{offer help, guidance,} \\ \text{or commitment} \end{array} \right\}$$

Color: Red is the international color for "stop." It signals important or dangerous issues that need to be discussed and mitigated.

Symbol: ! The exclamation point indicates "Hey! This is important!" Although not yet an international symbol, the exclamation point is creeping onto keyboards around the world.

Ask for help and action agents to solve Criticals.

When your stakeholders identify Critical issues, you not only need to understand the change they require but also to explain the help you will need to make that change effective. Stakeholders can provide documentation, remove obstacles, introduce you to influencers, or take other actions to ensure that the change is successful. Stakeholders should invest time or resources to fix the Critical issues.

Even if you can resolve the Critical issues yourself, with no help from your stakeholders, you can express a need for their feedback after you've solved the problem. Seeking their input and approval on the solution ensures that you're on the same page, you understood the problem, and you share a commitment to solve it.

In real life

One afternoon, an employee shocked me.

She quit.

I couldn't imagine how she could be upset with the work environment.

She could choose her hours.

She worked from home on one simple task: print pages for our records.

The Indiana University web team paid by the hour.

A perfect job for an undergraduate student who didn't need to tax her brain cells outside of class. She mindlessly printed and waited. And she got paid. What more could she want?

I needed to know whether I, her supervisor, provoked her resignation.

She explained that she enjoyed working from home, but couldn't afford to do the work. "Paper and print cartridges are too expensive," she said.

With those costs, she wasn't making any money.

I could have fixed the problem, if she had shared it with me. We had funds to reimburse her or we could have networked her computer to a campus printer.

We had options.

But we lost her because she didn't ask for help solving her Critical financial problem. She just assumed no one could help pay for paper and cartridges.

> **A note for grammar gurus:**
> For simplicity, the *C* category uses Critical as a noun instead of an adjective. Criticalness, the noun form of critical, just doesn't convey the intent of someone providing vital, urgent, or imperative feedback. Throughout the text, you'll see Critical or even Criticals.

I learned that every person has a different point of view and people higher in the organization may have the exact tools or resources you need.

Don't fear asking for help.

Uncover the intended impact of fixing the Criticals.

Fixing a Critical issue, especially late in the product life cycle, will require an investment in time, cost, or communication (and may result in delaying a product launch). When you understand the intention behind fixing the Critical issue, you may identify additional partners who are willing to split the cost of the investment or make the investment themselves.

If the intent is to avoid legal risk, you may find that your top executives accept the risk or can delay the launch of your design until the issue has been resolved by your team, tested with users, and approved by your legal department.

If the intent is to leverage a business opportunity, you may find that other parts of the organization will align to your work. Or perhaps amplify it at a marketing event.

If the intent is to decrease support calls, you may find that your contact center is willing to run a small test to see how many calls your design may cause. They may be willing to mitigate the risks by playing an announcement when your customers are on hold.

Essentially, if you can uncover partners who share your intent, you may uncover multiple options for resolving the issue beyond your deliverable's scope.

In real life

Imagine being the underdog in a corporation. Your product has to prove its viability to the decision makers. With minimal access to resources, your team must be scrappy and innovative. WARTS are the norm.

Unfortunately, when you feel like you're the underdog, you act like the underdog.

You may feel obligated to make assumptions about your partners and their goals.

As we built our case to iterate the search experience for Amazon, we assumed we'd be begging to get on the Search team's roadmap.

Search is core. They managed a multiyear backlog.

We assumed our foremost need would barely measure as a minor wish to them.

We based our mockup on a simple-to-code solution that would suffice our target audience of business customers. We intentionally designed to the bare bones. We didn't think we had any leverage to ask the core team to accommodate our small request.

The Search team reviewed our design.

I swear they laughed.

They explored our Suggestion with Questions to reveal the real Critical we craved. They wondered why we would settle.

Then we learned how our solution could also apply to other teams' needs, an unintentional value. We had partners we didn't even know existed.

Don't assume Criticals are difficult to resolve.

Our comfortable reaction to a Critical issue may be resistance or doubt. But not all Critical issues entail a laborious overhaul. Some involve low-hanging fruit that could be fixed within the given constraints.

Rather than assume Critical issues are difficult to resolve, listen to the complete explanation. Don't risk spending more time reacting and arguing than fixing the actual problem.

In real life

Here's an example from outside the user experience domain. Our electrical inspector needed to examine our new breaker boxes for our little blue cottage in Washington State.

We had fished the electrical wiring ourselves, crawling through the attic and pushing rope and wire down the walls to our new outlets. We just had to pass the wire down from the attic to install the electrical panel in the home's addition. Gravity and a staple gun took care of the rest.

We confidently walked the inspector, with his clipboard, overalls, and butt set, to the electrical panel.

Our hearts sank.

We failed his inspection.

We hadn't labelled the breakers correctly.

We quickly rearranged the stickers. Voilà! The Critical issue disappeared.

Summarize the Criticals and share their status.

Stakeholders' expectations are frequently loftier for Critical items than Suggestions, Questions, or Accidents. They want confidence that you've understood their feedback, that you will act, and that you will distribute the solution.

You can meet these expectations by making the status of each Critical transparent, especially any issues identified late in the life cycle. The closer the team is to launching the product to customers, the higher the stakes are for the stakeholders.

You can calm their nerves by scheduling a follow-up meeting shortly after the SQUACK session. Even if you have not determined the solution yet, seeing that the meeting has been scheduled can effectively prevent stakeholders from worrying and repeatedly querying you about what's happening.

By the way, before revealing your solution to all the stakeholders, you may want to socialize your solution with each stakeholder individually. Then they can successively endorse it to the others.

In real life

As we move through the life cycle of a product, our team provides a more formal status report that details the progress for mitigating Critical issues. We track each Critical with columns for the owner, resolution, deadline, and status. We intentionally add more information under different circumstances. If we are struggling to remove obstacles or failing to make progress, we add the date that the Critical was identified.

That additional transparency drives accountability. Fact based.

No arguments.

No emotion.

Just reality.

K FOR KUDOS

Definition: Praise or gratitude.

Formula:

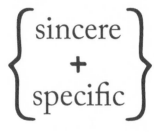

$$\left\{ \begin{array}{c} \text{sincere} \\ + \\ \text{specific} \end{array} \right\}$$

Color: Kudos are represented by blue, which traditionally evokes loyalty, trust, and understanding.

Symbol: ✱ The asterisk is a stand-in for earning a five-star review that describes specific reasons why you and your team earned the customer's respect and gratitude.

Anticipate and prepare your response to Kudos.

You may be apprehensive about hearing compliments and Kudos. You might not know how to respond and fear sounding arrogant if you accept compliments too readily. Remember, you deserve the spotlight and you can prepare a genuine and gracious response.

A note for grammar gurus: While some dictionaries have accepted *kudo* as the singular form of kudos, some grammarians argue that *kudo* is not even a word. I have gravitated toward using Kudo as the singular form of Kudos in the SQUACK feedback formula and throughout this book.

Practicing your reaction can help you avoid undermining your stakeholders' compliment with a dismissive "Ah, really, it was no big deal" or "I was just lucky." These comments can actually encourage your stakeholders to avoid giving you authentic Kudos in the future. Don't let them assume you're not using your hard-earned expertise.

Role-play your acceptance phrase.

Look at yourself in the mirror.

Imagine hearing someone compliment your work.

Watch your smile appear.

Say "Thank you for the compliment" or "Thank you for noticing."

Continue smiling and just be quiet. Let the SQUACKer speak next, if you can do so without feeling awkward.

If you're receiving an award, practice accepting the physical item in your left hand. You will want to shake hands with the person congratulating you, without feeling flustered as you move the item to your other hand. This is one situation in which being left-handed is a benefit: it'll be easier to reach out for the trophy with your dominant hand and then shake with your right hand. Practice receiving your well-deserved trophy without juggling it.

In real life

I am terrible at accepting Kudos. I tend to shirk off gratitude as "no big deal" and "anyone could have done (whatever you, dear Kudos giver, has appreciated)."

It's offensive to deflect or even ricochet back to the SQUACKer, "I couldn't have done it without your support." It sounds artificial.

And then it sounds crass when I catch my gut deflecting the gratitude: "Wait, let me rephrase that. Thank you for showing appreciation."

Instead, I pause when someone shows appreciation for my work. I focus on smiling, and then blinking once. I've discovered that by forcing the normally involuntary eyeblink, my facial muscles relax and my smile emerges naturally. Then I simply say, "Thank you."

Savor your moment in the spotlight.

Before your SQUACK review, take a few seconds to savor the work you and your teammates have completed. Be grateful for the insights you've gathered and the iterations you've made.

Consider which aspect deserves the most cheers because it solved a particularly prickly problem, provided a gratifying opportunity, heightened the expertise of multiple teammates, or seized the most intelligence to decipher. For whatever reason you are proud, Kudo yourself and your team. Consider revealing your proud moments to your stakeholders when you introduce the deliverable to them.

In real life

I habitually ask the team to describe what aspect of their work merits a prominent spot in their professional portfolio. I want to encourage them to take pride in their craft and tell me how I can elevate their work.

Before I ask for SQUACK feedback of my own work, I mentally assess what changes I should make. I think about how likely I would choose that work for a prominent spot in my portfolio or my stash of work samples.

I then consider what challenges I let become obstacles.

Did I sabotage my own work by not making persuasive arguments?

Accept constraints too readily?

Fail to engage with others who could have improved it if I had only asked?

Ideally, all our work should merit spotlight attention. I hope all your work is worthy of a story and you save a copy for future discussions and bragging rights.

As a manager, I focus on the impact my coaching, mentoring, and SQUACKing have on the team. I haven't played a maker role for a while, so I have learned to give my folders meaningful names that speak to the contributions I make to teams: Correct Assumptions, Risky Recommendations, Building a Leadership Bench, Process Optimizations, Persuading Leaders, Significant Decisions.

While I name the files for sharing with other people, I name the folders for myself.

Then I screenshot my expanded Documents folder.

Reviewing that list of files quarterly has become my self-Kudo process.

Create a Kudos archive.

Remember, at the end of a SQUACK session, to collect any Kudo sticky notes, write the stakeholder and project names on it, and add any context that will help you remember why you received that Kudo. If your SQUACK session is remote, take a screenshot of the thread or digital sticky notes.

Then create a stash of them in your desk drawer or on your computer. Seriously, take that time to record the details: who, what, and when. Then, when you need a pick-me-up, you can read through the previous Kudos.

Reminisce whenever and wherever you want.

In real life

Although most of mine have faded, I cherish each Kudo note I have tucked away over the years. I have Hallmark thank-you cards, a sticky note scrawled with a star, and creative drawings from designers.

I retrieve the folder and paw through its contents when the imposter syndrome seeps into my psyche.

One note succinctly says, "Raccoon!" It's cryptic. The employee meant she appreciated how I notoriously poke around, seeking opportunities and planting seeds to harvest later. That note says my raccoon resilience can locate opportunities hidden from others.

All those compliments about my style and expertise rush back when I see that one-word Kudo.

Consider whether or not to accept the Kudos.

Your success, aesthetics, or ingenuity may surprise your stakeholders. Maybe they can't imagine that you intentionally enabled a benefit they see in your work. You may find that when a stakeholder assumes a benefit was unintentional or even a mistake, your patience may lead to an authentic and heartfelt Kudo.

You could point out that you did indeed anticipate that delight, or you could ask yourself whether you need to call that attention to yourself.

In real life

My father, an architect, renovated the Immaculate Conception Cathedral for Pope John Paul's visit to Denver for World Youth Day, 1993. Dad promised me a tour of his work. I climbed the catwalk, lumbered up the bell tower, and admired the spires and windows. I loved gazing over to the State Capitol Building from inside the cathedral.

A dignified voice called to my dad: "Harvey, Harvey! Do you see this? It's incredible!" A man wearing a red skullcap pointed at the reflection of the stained glass windows on the street level.

"This brings the church onto the street, where everyone can see it: the details, the colors, the saints. An amazing chance."

In reality, my father intentionally specified the protective glass (with a transparent street-side barrier to protect the antique stained glass on the interior). Not only did its strength withstand vandalism, hail, and debris, its clarity let the sun shine through. He knew the stained-glass images would replicate on the sidewalk below.

Dad didn't anticipate a sunny morning while I visited his work site at the same time the archbishop strolled down Colfax Avenue. The reflection embellished the street. My father just relished in his reaction. This fortuitous "accident" was absolutely intentional.

My father treaded into the background so that his work could be admired. No need to heighten his architectural expertise.

Pardon any Kudo procrastinators.

Stakeholders may only remember to give you a Kudo as an afterthought, if at all. Don't let their procrastination or rudeness block your basking in all the iterations you've made to arrive at your solution.

Business challenges never cease, and your stakeholders are likely burdened with many worries themselves. Leaders fret about profits and losses and stress about the bottom line. So, when you receive an afterthought Kudo that is generic or almost forgotten, don't let it bother you.

Appreciate a Kudo, no matter how it arrives: early or late, shallow or authentic. You deserve the appreciation for your deliverable. Relish in your work, reflect on it, and appreciate it yourself. Choose to appreciate your work yourself.

In real life

The main reason SQUACK ends with Kudo is because I needed a strong mnemonic to remember to thank the team, reinforce the attributes and skills that extend beyond the immediate deliverable, and simply be grateful.

Part of my job is to eliminate obstacles before the team needs to tackle them. Sometimes this means I breeze through the present deliverable and immediately predict hazards that must be cleared. Once I have confidence in the current deliverable, I move quickly to the next challenge

Frequently, I fail to acknowledge today's accomplishments. I have had to teach myself to stop and appreciate the current work. I still slip up and only acknowledge the work after I have made Suggestions, asked Questions, circled Accidents, and raised Critical implications.

My Kudos tend to arrive delayed. Sincere, but overdue.

How important are timely Kudos?

I've been asked why timeliness is not part of the Kudos formula. While a timely Kudos is ideal, people value a *thank you* that specifically calls out their contribution more than an immediate, but generic, thanks. A simple, 'great job', while appreciated, lacks the punch of a *thank you* that describes the reason why the work was exemplary. This rule applies days later. Even months later. Heck, even decades later.

In Real Life

My college internship in the Colorado House of Representatives was most rewarding when a legislator stopped by in-person to thank me for a speech I had written. His audience had applauded him and he wanted to return that accolade to me. It was the first time an adult stranger had thanked me for my work. When I reached out to express my thanks to him, now years later, I learned that his family was not aware of the speech nor the news article that captured that moment. They already knew he was an inspiration; my Kudos just expanded that legacy even more.

So, send that note, make that phone call, plan that visit. It's not too late.

LET SQUACK
TAKE FLIGHT
ON YOUR TEAM

Introducing your team to a new method, like SQUACK, can feel like you're rebelling. Afterall, people tend to enjoy randomly sharing their reactions, opinions and ideas, without thinking much about how others will act on their feedback.

SQUACK leverages common sense categories that people can easily understand. The challenge is remembering to apply the categories.

Luckily, you can adapt the SQUACK approach to align to your team's existing processes, vocabulary, and ceremonies. Then, remind your stakeholders, partners, and managers to use the categories as part of their traditional feedback activities. I have uncovered and evolved the following best practices when preparing, facilitating, and acting on feedback sessions.

Clarify when each SQUACK category is (and isn't) helpful.

While you should be eager to hear all SQUACK feedback, you need to set expectations for which types are most relevant based on the stage of your project. Whether you follow Agile or Waterfall; Double Diamond, ADDIE, Six Sigma, or whatever, Design Thinking, you likely explore, iterate, develop, and then implement the user experience when you have confidence in your design or have met the minimum requirements.

In early phases, you typically brainstorm Suggestions with minimal concern about careless Accidents. Later, you focus solely on hearing about those Accidents and any Critical feedback that must be resolved before implementation.

Here's a simplified product life cycle that assumes your deliverables iterate from low fidelity to high fidelity. You'll want to let your SQUACKers know where you are in the life cycle and remind them what type of feedback is most helpful to you. I recommend updating the terminology to match your team's process, so they can simply adopt the SQUACK feedback formula without having to learn a new process as well.

Stage 1: Exploration abounds. The UX team analyzes users, interviews stakeholders, and creates low-fidelity assets such as storyboards, scenarios, and flow diagrams. Scope has not been decided.

Suggestions	are valuable and actionable
Questions	can clarify the intent
User Signal	informs the concept and direction
Accidents	are not important (nothing is final)
Criticals	should be raised, the earlier the better
Kudos	are welcomed

Stage 2: Revisions proceed. The UX team creates wireframes, prototypes, and other medium- to high-fidelity assets and iterates them based on usability test results and other insights.

Suggestions	are welcomed because scope is still expandable
Questions	help set context
User Signal	likely includes usability testing
Accidents	will be fixed
Criticals	need to be shared
Kudos	are appreciated

Stage 3: Development begins. The team commits to the scope and timeline based on the successful iterations. The prototype morphs into working code.

Suggestions	beyond the current scope or that risk the established timeline will need to be punted to a future release
Questions	likely explore the effort as if it were completed
User Signal	should support the design rationale and storytelling
Accidents	need prioritization (some may not be fixed before launch)
Criticals	require tradeoff considerations and possible mitigation
Kudos	are only appropriate if sufficient time exists (Accidents and Criticals are more important)

Stage 4: Customers react. The team conducts beta releases until real customers react to the real product.

Suggestions	are scoped and prioritized for the next version
Questions	should explore impact, opportunities, and metrics
User Signal	should holistically measure success / failure through data, feedback, and research
Accidents	are prioritized for future work
Criticals	become top-priority items to fix
Kudos	are welcomed and measurable with actual results

In real life

When we created wireframes of our chatbot that provided financial guidance and advice, our stakeholders often made Suggestions. They worried that our conversational bubbles, despite being written in a friendly tone, were too long and drawn out. The pages seemed lengthy as we scrolled down on the overhead display in our conference rooms. Stakeholders routinely wanted us to eliminate the entire chatbot experience. Our confidence was justified; we'd explored user needs and iterated our design based on usability tests with actual customers. Numerous rounds of testing, iterating, repeating.

So, during our midpoint review, we reminded our stakeholders that our product intended to earn trust through a conversational design that built a relationship with our customers. We summarized how we responded to key usability findings and then we invited our stakeholders to experience the chatbot for themselves on a higher-fidelity design. This time, rather than watching us scroll over the chat bubbles, they would view and tap the experience on their own devices.

Our design had evolved and now reflected the more authentic experience we wanted to deliver to our customers. We prepared to transition the design to the development phase.

After the stakeholders tapped through the experience, we asked them to SQUACK screen by screen, showing each chat bubble on the room's display. We collected Suggestions, answered Questions, and ultimately earned a memorable Kudo from one of the most skeptical techie folks in the room, Paul Reichlin: "Originally, I doubted this whole chatbot experience, Julie. But somehow, on my device, it worked. I found myself wanting to respond just to discover what the chatbot would advise me to do next. Dammit. It worked!"

PLAN A SQUACK SESSION

Provide abundant context.

Do you juggle the details of one, two, three, or more design projects? Keeping the details organized, at least in your head, probably comes naturally to you. Or maybe you create mental shortcuts—naming conventions for file names? Notes? Whiteboard sketches?

You likely also know the WARTS of your design: its weaknesses, adaptations, risks, tradeoffs, and shortcomings. And you realize what constraints caused those WARTS (typically deadline, financial, or resource constraints). Sharing the WARTS with your stakeholders can compel them to alleviate the constraints

But to understand the implications of changing or eliminating your constraints, your stakeholders need context. They will not likely recall your constraints; they may have 10x or 100x more projects muddying their brains.

For example, they may have digital design responsibility as well as employee (hiring, performance management, budget concerns), security (physical, digital, risk management, compliance, legal), platform (app, website, hybrid, marketing, service, retention), integration (internal, third-party, geographically separated operations), profit and loss (earnings, capital expenses, dividends, reporting to the board of directors) physical locations (blueprints, security systems, insurance), and numerous other looming accountabilities.

Want more insights about the brain capacity of your stakeholders? Scrutinize your company's annual report. You may recognize where your work aligns to the overarching strategy. It may just be a fraction of the overall report (and therefore a fraction of your stakeholders' time). Yet that fraction still consumes 100% of your work brain.

How can you help your stakeholders untangle the gray matter in their brains? Convey your context, clearly and comprehensively.

Context may include:

- the project title in official and familiar words as merited,
- the audience/users,
- the project phase, and
- decisions (either pending or determined).

You don't want to test their patience with a lengthy diatribe. You also don't want to risk being so brief that they don't recognize their opportunity to help. Providing adequate context for stakeholders requires leaning more toward their need to know over your desire to tell.

Who knows? Maybe providing proactive context may entice your stakeholders to attend your SQUACK session instead of an alluring but conflicting meeting or even devote their free time to participate in your sessions. It wouldn't be the first time SQUACK became a team's favorite ceremony.

In real life

Helping teams understand the importance of providing context about their status and design rationale is a recurring coaching point for me.

Across every industry and every company.

The format for setting context varies from company to company and team to team. Sometimes even stakeholder to stakeholder. The context itself is fairly routine. The method of delivery varies.

Email announcement: We predictably answer the 5 Ws in the meeting invitation itself: what the project is, who the target audience is, when we expect to launch it, where we are in the process, and why they should SQUACK it. That last item—essentially, what's in it for them—typically divulges itself when I announce what areas we are still debating or what constraints are hazarding us trouble.

Meeting: We may include the word *SQUACK* in the meeting invitation and display the definitions either in the room on a poster or table tent or as the opening slide for remote meetings (see squackfeedback.com to access these resources). Stakeholders can ask me to refresh their memory about SQUACK or I can proactively remind them. I prefer pre-emptively preventing basic process questions.

FAQ: We may write a comprehensive FAQ document and share it with our stakeholders in advance of the

SQUACK session. Either they can read it at their leisure or we can read it as a team before SQUACKing begins.

Context-setting slide: We may provide a context page or slide that lists the known constraints and explains the steps completed to date. Our intent is to describe why the team has confidence in our deliverable and how the stakeholders could minimize any WARTS by adjusting timelines or other constraints. The key is to be transparent. We typically don't walk through or speak to the slide, but we make sure it's visible.

Cover sheet: We may include a cover sheet at the beginning of our SQUACK reviews to clarify the status of our deliverable. We point out whether our legal team has reviewed the content, it is considered a draft, or it's been through the final edit. This context indicates what type of Accidents to expect. When all the quality-checking steps are complete, we should not have any Accidents and we would appreciate our SQUACKers discreetly bringing any remaining errors to our attention. If we haven't completed those steps, our SQUACKers should anticipate that things aren't perfect. We might be embarrassed if Accidents exist, but we are not surprised if they do. Marc, one of the lawyers I've worked with, once confessed to me that he relies on seeing whether the compliance box has been checked or not. If it's checked, he knows he's

already seen this deliverable and he knows he'd better not change his mind!

Hand-drawn whiteboard process: Sometimes we may need to remind folks about other opportunities they've had to SQUACK and contribute. To avoid rants about every detail, I may draw a timeline on the whiteboard.

The subliminal message is that UX doesn't mysteriously fabricate designs; we follow an iterative process with multiple SQUACK critiques.

Ensuring that everyone is on the same page enables the team to explore options and have deeper conversations about their confidence and opportunities.

kickoff 4 Interviews iterations   1st SQUACK

I may ask the team: "If we didn't have any time constraints (or we removed restrictions), what do you wish you could accomplish?" or "What are the shortcomings of your deliverable—what value can you envision if we alleviated that constraint?"

Our stakeholders may then exclaim: "If it only takes one or two more sprints to produce that value, let's do it!"

today

usability tests   iterations   2nd SQUACK   design freeze

Take a deep breath.

Focusing on your breathing before your SQUACK session will naturally calm you. That focus takes your mind off the details of the deliverable that you've sweated over. That focus also helps you consider what is important: relishing the fact that you are about to become the center of attention. People are going to focus on making your deliverable better.

Take those deep breaths, relax, and relish in your moment.

In real life

Expecting a scientific reference regarding the value of deep breathing? Your favorite search engine can lead you to a plausible reason why deep breathing works. But why not just try it for yourself? Try taking a breath after each word you type in the search box:

"Does" *(inhale, hold, exhale)*

"deep" *(inhale, hold, exhale)*

"breathing" *(inhale, hold, exhale)*

"really" *(inhale, hold, exhale)*

"help" *(inhale, hold, exhale)*

Imagine how great you'd feel after 10 deep breaths!

Detach yourself from your work.

Remember, people's reactions are not personal. Opinions may feel personal to you, but the other people are merely reacting to your results, not to you. They aren't as invested as you are. So, take the opportunity to SQUACK your own deliverable as if you weren't invested. See your own work with a fresh set of eyes and articulate your own Suggestions and Critical changes. And, seriously, congratulate yourself with Kudos too.

You know how you solved the challenging problems. Recall which aspects required the most consideration and exploration. Remember, the work you did to prevent a problem is probably invisible to others. Kudo yourself because you prevented users from ever experiencing that struggle.

In real life

One way to detach myself from the work is to recall my first raw, uninformed, unrefined iteration. The scrappy version before planning research, collecting feedback, considering tradeoffs, and discovering constraints. I save a version of the raw original of all my work, whether it's a website, a plan, a report, a dashboard, or even a book.

Sometimes I retain just a photo of my whiteboard. I want to retain the shallow "before" experience along with the iterations needed to make the deliverable market worthy.

Why do I retain rough work? Because I need to remember the evolutions and journeys I took from that original assumption-informed version to the final user-, expertise-, and SQUACK-informed version of my work. I consider my real contribution is the thought leadership needed to expose and react to constraints and hypotheticals.

If I've done my job well, SQUACKers are excluded from my melee and discoveries. They enjoy the end result without sloshing through the swamp themselves.

Be transparent about the status of previous Criticals.

Prepare to discuss how the Critical items have been resolved or are underway. If you need your stakeholders' action to resolve the Critical items, know what help you need and be ready to ask for it. When your stakeholders designate their feedback as Critical, they want to see it resolved and are willing to help.

Make sure you understand the feedback before you disagree with its criticality, because Critical feedback should be rare and well defined.

In real life

Our compliance partners raised multiple, supposedly Critical feedback items, one of which was designating the font sizes of our disclaimers, including a 48-pt font size, on our mobile app.

We listened to the feedback, paraphrased it back to show we understood it, and provided an FAQ for how we resolved each Critical issue during the next SQUACK review. We included screenshots and then asked our partners about whether other options sufficiently met their needs and the legal requirements. We transparently gave our partners choices and helped them understand our rationale for choosing a smaller font size.

One of the lawyers admitted that the regulations can be interpreted in different ways and he appreciated that we gave him options. With that discussion, we truly became partners in delivering both a legal and usable experience.

Seek feedback long before you have the "right" design.

Thought experiment: how can you effectively negotiate with a bear emerging from hibernation? He's been unconscious deep inside his cave. As he lumbers out, he's focused exclusively on his own survival, and he'll deliciously devour any morsel his nostrils uncover. You may provoke him if you get in his way.

Sure, you only want to help him find the hackberries down by the river or warn him about the pack of wolves that have discovered his scent. (You know, you only want to share constructive survival feedback.)

Now, imagine meeting Jun Ior, a designer who's been isolated for weeks, focused solely on creating a flawless design. Jun is confident that when he's done, a masterpiece will be revealed and deep and meaningful accolades will be bestowed upon the work. Everyone will simply devour it with appreciation. It's perfect. But you want to provide guardrails to ensure a positive impact and steer Jun away from designer danger zones. (You know, you only want to share constructive design feedback.)

Neither the hibernating bear nor the isolated designer will tolerate anyone who obstructs their way, even if the feedback could reveal a better flow, full of honey and berries.

Avoiding stakeholders is going to backfire. When Jun waits until the work is ready or done, the stakeholders can't contribute to his success. They can't steer him away from missteps, danger zones, and cliffs. They won't feel invested in Jun's success if he hasn't invited their participation.

Designing is an interactive sport. You need others to throw, wedge, and stuff their ideas in with yours. Our job as designers is to make sense of everyone's concepts, concerns, wishes, wants, wonders, desires, fears, and ambitions. We leverage our expertise and judgment to frame that chaos into a consumable format so that everyone has a shared visual to stare at, chagrin, and admire. That common reference can then be improved and overhauled under the guidance of the expert who made sense of all the ideas: you.

Notice:
I'm not suggesting you design in public. You need concentration time to express your ideas on paper or in pixels. Your outputs need to be shared. Your steps are mental and may not be visible. You definitely don't need anyone standing over your shoulder ordering you around. That's a painful culture that stifles the best designs.

You may fear getting feedback that you don't want or merely disagree with. It's always better to get that feedback early so that you can prepare your design rationale, your storytelling, or your data collection to overcome those disagreeable ideas. Let SQUACKers inform your initial low-fidelity designs so that you can course correct early, while you can still appreciate their Suggestions and accommodate changes.

In real life

I always worry when someone has been hibernating with their designs. It's one of the first habits I breach when I start managing a new team. The first week on the job, I casually stroll through the office looking for evidence of my new team's design work.

Are the walls plastered with our mockups and ideas?

What versions are hanging up: only picture-perfect, laminated posters of our final designs? Or sketches on whiteboards with doodles, notes, and question marks?

Are the designs visible to everyone or are they locked behind security doors in the design studio?

I want to understand why designs are hidden (they typically are, especially if the team has been without a manager). When the designs become public, what is the reaction? Has anyone been humiliated or made uncomfortable for their decisions?

I want to mitigate the root cause for not being transparent and ensure that we have a framework, à la SQUACK, to make the feedback more actionable and less harsh.

At Capital One, designs required picturesque and poised perfection. The culture tended to avoid sharing work in progress, unless it could be framed proudly.

Meanwhile, at Microsoft, we tended to create design caves, where we shared work with the internal team only. In both cases, I worked with the teams to expose their work while it was in progress. We then worked together to help stakeholders understand which types of feedback would help throughout the life cycle.

It requires grit. When we share our designs early, stakeholders buy into the design from the beginning and then proudly see their thumbprint within our success. Let's hear others' ideas without overreacting, appreciate the chance to share goals and work together, and embrace getting our hands dirty and our brains exhausted.

FACILITATE A SQUACK SESSION

Display the SQUACK formula and the link to your work.

Not everyone is punctual, so expect that some folks may join your meeting late. You can help them catch up by displaying instructions on-screen or on a whiteboard. For example:

Welcome to our SQUACK session for our new mobile app

Categorize your feedback accordingly:

Suggestion	Question	User Signal	Accident	Critical	Kudos
A comment or idea based on opinions or personal experiences.	An area that needs clarity or exploration.	Data, feedback, or research that spurs a compelling Suggestion or authentic Kudo.	A typo, copy and paste error, misalignment, or math mistake.	A problem that must be resolved because of the potential business risk or customer pain.	Praise or gratitude.

We start SQUACKing in 04:30

- **Access the wireframe:** mobile.design.url
- **Where to SQUACK:** in the meeting chat
- **Start your feedback with a letter:** S-Q-U-A-C-K
- **Design phase:** Exploration abounds (we appreciate your Suggestions and Questions most; no need to identify Accidents)

Page 116 will help you determine which SQUACK categories are most helpful throughout the product life cycle.

In real life

I am notoriously late for meetings. I used to blame the distance between meetings, moving from one building, floor, or conference room to another. Now that we're working remotely, I still arrive late. So I always appreciate having a few minutes to SQUACK a deliverable privately before the discussion gets started.

Some teams even send the deliverable in advance (though there's no guarantee that everyone will read it until the SQUACK meeting).

Kudo your stakeholders.

Thank your stakeholders for sharing their time, being thoughtful, and learning to SQUACK. Your sincere gratitude goes a long way toward building trust, respect, and credibility, especially if you mention how their feedback has made you think differently or exposed a gap.

They'd love to hear how their insights influence your design.

In real life

Stakeholders, especially those at the top of an organization, typically don't hear positive comments and rarely receive acknowledgments for their work and their ideas.

It's true.

Their butts are on the line for every decision, even those they didn't make and may not understand. They have ultimate accountability but likely lack insight into every detail.

They feel the weight of their decisions, especially in terms of the livelihood of their employees.

Their days are focused on fixing or explaining problems.

They are preoccupied with legal, business, technical, political, and personality challenges.

They relish seeing deliverables in progress.

Participating in design sessions is an indulgence.

Hearing appreciation is rare.

When they have fought their way to the top, they may be weary of the constant battle. Someone is always willing to take their place. They may feel insecure and are expected to know everything, predict the unforeseen, and explain negative results. They rejoice when the metrics are better than expected, but they know what to expect next: a new precedent and a new expectation that they'll have to meet. The work never ends. If the targets are exceeded, they get reset.

Everyone expects more and more from them. Leaders are only human. Hearing Kudos for sharing their insights and striving to use SQUACK is welcoming. Even better, seeing you act on their feedback is simply gratifying.

Acknowledge the whole team.

Seldom can a person authentically claim to discover or create an entire innovation. As Isaac Newton wrote in 1675, "If I have seen further it is by standing on the shoulders of giants." So, Kudo the giants who came before you to soften the mood and spur conciliatory discussions.

For example, film credits traditionally list not only movie stars, directors, and producers, but anyone who contributed to the collaborative effort: the grip, the best boy, the bartenders, the caterers, the typist who keyed 10+ minutes of scrolling names.

Show gratitude to folks who contributed or SQUACKed your deliverable, because teamwork is essential to our own success. Showing gratitude to others is not a weakness. Your gratitude actually reinforces your confidence in the work.

Stakeholders may forget they've SQUACKed your work in the past. A thank-you slide or a mention reminds them they've provided feedback already. Seeing their name boosts their acceptance and accountability. In other words, the reason the design is the way it is today is partially because of their previous SQUACKing.

In real life

Here are two examples that acknowledge unusual and invisible contributors.

Wilfrid Hodges, author of *Model Theory: Encyclopedia of Mathematics and Its Application*, acknowledged unusual contributors: "If this book...is not a success, I dedicate it to the burglars in Boulder, Colorado, who broke into our house and stole a television, two typewriters, my wife Helen's engagement ring, and several pieces of cheese, somewhere about a third of the way through Chapter 8."

I'd like to credit the credit-less: Eddy Chandler, the forgotten actor. Eddy's name never appeared in any film credits. But he acted in 350 movies (no one knows the exact number, because, ahem, he was not credited). He appeared in *Gone with the Wind*, *You Can't Take It with You*, and *It Happened One Night* (yes, Academy Award–winning films). He got paid, but never got credit.

I imagine him being the first person in line as an extra in every film. His real job? Get up and take part. He must not have craved fame; he enjoyed participating. I imagine him, full of grit and diligence, contributing, however and whenever.

So, here are the Kudos to people like Eddy for their resilience and persistence. Way to go, ya'll!

Designate the SQUACK category yourself or use the echo ruse.

If stakeholders fail to designate their feedback as a Suggestion, Critical, Question, et cetera, paraphrase them and assume which category they intended. They can always correct you.

If you're not certain what the stakeholder intended, repeat her last three words (or a significant phrase that she said) and then pause. If you end this 'echo' with a slightly higher tone, the stakeholder will likely think you're struggling to understand what she means and then she'll naturally clarify her intent.

In real life

I typically paraphrase my stakeholders' comments so that they know I have understood them. I either echo the last few words they said or clarify with "that sounds like…" For example: "That sounds like a Suggestion, because you would like to set a default that would apply to 90% of our audience."

Then, once I confirm their Suggestion, I can follow up with a Question: "Can our data predict when the default question won't apply? Then maybe we could just let 90% of our users skip the question entirely?" By showing how I intended to use their Suggestion, I open the door for further discussion and exploration.

First and foremost, the stakeholders feel heard, inviting us to partner with them on a better solution.

When I introduced SQUACK to my peers, one of the product managers, a native English speaker, doubted people would know what *kudos* means. He voiced a Suggestion to find a better word for Kudo. I helped him formulate his opinion as a Suggestion (yes, it involved a small grammar lesson) and thanked him for speaking up.

Afterward, I chose to ignore his Suggestion.

I decided not to act, because SQUACK is memorable with Kudos at the end. And I just believed people can learn new words. I was right. Within six months, our multidisciplinary team expressed Kudos via email, in person, in thank-you notes, during meetings, on sticky notes, through town halls, and even in fireside chats with executives.

Reformulate opinions and insults.

Suggestions are actionable; opinions are not. Essentially, opinions don't matter. Even customer reviews don't matter. Sure, negative reviews can hurt your feelings. I get it. But when you hear or read negative opinions, review your Kudos archive (see page 108) to remind yourself about your exemplary work and balance the perceptions in your own head.

Then decide to be bold. Ignore the opinions and carry on.

If a stakeholder I'll call Egoma Niac routinely expresses negative opinions about Jun Ior's work, you can compel Egoma to stop. Reinforce the Suggestion formula and raise authentic Kudos for Jun's work.

It'll require courage.

In hindsight, you will not regret speaking up. Bullies, who magnify themselves by berating others, never compare favorably to defenders, who validate, endorse, and congratulate the hard workers who find themselves victimized by hurtful comments and actions. People will remember how you made them feel, so lavish your Kudos.

In real life

Although I typically encourage team members to think positive thoughts, I sometimes find my own inspiration differently. As I prepare for a SQUACK session, I recall how I've overcome tough situations.

I may recall walking through my deliverable with one of the biggest jerks I've ever worked with. He had an opinion about everything; no element existed beyond his callous remark.

He's the guy who, when I dared to ask him about a decision he'd made, launched a 3-inch-thick book across the room.

At me.

I had to duck.

I'd just graduated from college. He was a senior staff member. He's the one who also said to me, "You just can't send a woman to do a man's job." And here I thought neanderthals were extinct.

He's the worst character I can imagine. So, as I prepare for SQUACK sessions, I remind myself about that day. It's kind of a badge of honor today.

I know now that I don't need to respond to derogatory and deriding opinions about my deliverables (or about my gender, my expertise, or myself). I don't act on opinions. I consider Suggestions to improve my deliverables. I channel the courage and confidence to act only on things that matter, and I only listen to voices I want to hear and not the squawking of people who want to intimidate, annoy, or bully.

How did I respond to getting the book thrown at me?

I focused on my breathing.

Then I rephrased my request. Simple. Stupid.

I waited. Tolerantly.

He eventually answered.

I didn't say another word.

I merely walked away, clasping his book in my hand.

Establish common terminology.

Paraphrase the Suggestion in your own words while minimizing your own discipline's jargon, even if that means you need to alter your terms. Try to establish a shared terminology with the other disciplines in the SQUACK session. By adopting others' terms or fusing theirs with your own, you build rapport with your stakeholders and help them recognize the overlap of one another's expertise.

Talking about your stakeholders' needs in their language enables you to transparently translate their opinions into actionable Suggestions. It may take longer than you hope, but your diligence, agility, and translation will pay off.

In real life

When presenting a prototype to employees at Microsoft, I realized the attendees represented 52 countries and worked in nearly every time zone. It was a momentous event for me, an ego volcano: bombing the presentation would be a cancerous disaster but nailing it would cause a self-esteem eruption.

Our project had streamlined their sales process and updated their tools significantly. Ultimately, we changed the livelihood of every sales force employee. Gratefully, every attendee spoke English as either a first or second (or probably even third or fourth) language.

During the first review session, I introduced the top links as the "global nav bar." The employees referenced the global navigation links as "universal." Instead of correcting them or trying to change their thinking to mine, I used both terms interchangeably during the remaining reviews. When we created the training documents for new employees, I made sure our glossary definition for *global* included the synonym *universal.*

I had a blast and loved adjusting our terminology and presentation on the fly.

Celebrate and then diplomatically debunk historical assumptions.

Organizations may know about their users' bygone needs, expectations, approaches, and impressions. Stakeholders may unintentionally make assumptions and rely on their historical knowledge as they consider creating new experiences. Unfortunately, that knowledge may grow stale as competitors emerge, technologies evolve, and expectations change. Yesterday's loyal users may be antsy. As you research and iterate, ask your stakeholders when they last verified their user assumptions.

Your stakeholders may resist unveiling anything new, or you may both discover that you need to confirm whether user expectations have changed. In either case, you need to identify whether you can confidently reveal that users have changed or whether you need to be subtle in exposing new user needs. To effectively expose changes, you may need to research topics that tangentially overlap. Essentially, your users may expose their needs while you are researching other topics.

In real life

When managing the UX team that launched Office 365, my peers and I believed Microsoft's partner ecosystem would rebel against our company interacting directly with enterprise customers. That is, the independent software vendors (ISVs), who had built their businesses around helping companies deploy Microsoft products, would protest our entry into their business world. We braced for their gut-wrenching reactions during our software development reviews.

All our online services threatened their livelihood.

We prepared for aggressive feedback at the software design review with dozens of ISV leaders from around the world. We assumed rightly and wrongly. The companies either loudly protested our entrance or claimed a new value for their customers.

Our research enabled different relationships within our partner–customer ecosystem. We celebrated their existing success with them and urged them to pivot their value propositions.

Commit an intentional and correctable mistake.

Let the stakeholders express their value by pointing out mistakes you intentionally made. Let them relish catching the errors on your behalf.

Be mindful and respectful if you use this tactic to boost the value your stakeholders can provide. And never repeat the exact same Accident. If you make the same mistake multiple times, you'll invite more scrutiny of your deliverables.

When you can thank someone for finding a simple mistake, both of you feel good, because not only does your mistake get fixed, they helped you fix it. That appreciative reaction from you can further ensure that the conversation between the two of you continues.

In real life

At Los Alamos National Laboratory, we rampantly reorganized teams, groups, and divisions. I predominantly worked in the Chemical Science and Technology Division, aka the Chemistry Division, C-Division, or just Chemistry.

Someone in leadership always pointed out when I had the name wrong. The clarification was important to the leaders; I'm sure they argued with their peers about the name, the structure, the numbers, and the specifics of the

154

reorganization. They wanted credit for the excruciating minutiae they fought for. Luckily, fixing the Accident was simple; keeping up with the name changes was not. The leaders felt like champions when they could correct my mistake, reinforcing their hard-fought battle. I dutifully made the correction, lest I insult the battling leaders.

I've also used Accidents to identify supporters, neutralists, and detractors of my work.

Remember, I worked in the Chemistry Division, well known for lengthy chemical compounds and difficult-to-pronounce words (yes, the longest word in English is a chemical compound that stretches 189,000+ letters long).

To identify folks who respect you, try mispronouncing nuclear (as *nu-cu-ler*). People who care about your credibility and want to see you succeed will correct your pronunciation mistake.

After a presentation about the Nuclear group, I had three chemists tell me I mispronounced their name. I knew they supported my work and I knew they would provide honest feedback to me.

My mispronunciation revealed a bit about the folks I worked with.

Remember, Accidents can be advantageous.

Accidents can help you know whether people are paying attention to your work. If they don't notice an Accident, they may not care, may be distracted, or may not be detailed enough for the type of SQUACK review you need.

Or they may be too intimidated to tell you about your mistakes. It's like when you eat quiche at lunch and realize that evening that you have spinach caught in your teeth. You may discover your stakeholders are reticent or distracted if they fail to notice your errors.

In real life

My father, an architect, knew the power of making deliberate errors. He knew that subcontractors and suppliers would take shortcuts to avoid reading the tediously long architectural specifications. So he inserted made-up words and unexpected phrases within his specs.

He always knew when they didn't read his specifications, because they wouldn't comment on his "medifated" instructions. Silence on their part caused him to audit more closely.

For the record, my father would define his made-up words. *Medifated* meant premeditated fate; an intentional mistake intended to evoke a reaction.

And *enbabble* meant to enable others to babble because you want to avoid hurting their feelings or stepping on their toes. My father wanted his made-up words to join the *Oxford English Dictionary*. None of his terms has made it. We're still "anticihoping."

Be friendly without undermining your expertise.

As you're building rapport with stakeholders, partners, and peers, you need to genuinely understand their goals and realize their success is also your success. Business rapport, after all, involves being approachable, building trust, and adding your expert value. You need to stay firm to your conviction about the quality of your work and your obligation to employ your expertise. After all, your hiring manager fought to open your position.

She sought approval from her manager or the board of directors. She set expectations for the role and envisioned the impact a perfect candidate would have on the company. She budgeted and negotiated against other teams who needed to hire someone. She argued why she needed your role now, not later. She must defend her team and every role on it, for every backfill and new position.

She finessed the job description and argued where to advertise. She drowned in resumes and portfolios. She established the interview process, design problems, and instructions for the interviewers.

All before she met you.

She debriefed after every interview loop. She debated with HR, management, and finance about the salary to offer. Then she waited and prayed you'd accept. She considered counteroffers and backup offers to other possible candidates. She dreamed about your first assignment and what gaps you'd fill on her team.

All before you started.

She ordered or requested your equipment. Acquired security access, logons, and permissions. Scheduled your new-employee orientation. Conducted her own onboarding activities and introduced you to your teammates, partners, and stakeholders.

All before your first design review.

She's lucky to have you; you owe it to her to live up to the promises on your resume.

You have credibility and expertise. You may want to be amicable. Not bossy or arrogant. But if you say "I think" or "I feel," you're implying doubt, hesitation, or lack of conviction. Your manager wants you to have conviction. She knows your capabilities and potential.

So, make a friendly impression without undermining your abilities. Try meeting people before you need their feedback. Kick off your SQUACK session with a friendly banter or sincere gratefulness to the stakeholders for attending. Be personable so that you can showcase your expertise without dominating.

In real life

Jun Ior, a new member of the UX team at Microsoft, nervously rolled her eyes to the back of her head when she described her work to an audience of authority figures. If they asked Questions, she repeatedly began her answers with the words "I think."

I knew she knew the answers despite appearing alarmingly uncomfortable.

To Jun, an authority figure could be anyone for any reason. Culturally, she felt obligated to be nice, show respect, and avoid conflict. She had no experience working for an American company.

She had the UX experience and the expertise.

She just lacked the poise and persona of a corporate employee who could respectfully disagree and show conviction. I coached communication skills and Suggested that she present irrefutable facts, backed up with substantial data (she did not need to share the data, she just needed to know it existed).

This way, she could start with more conviction and less doubt.

She limited the words on each slide to 20 or fewer, so she could tell the story without merely reading the slides.

Once she warmed up presenting the facts, she relaxed. Instead of saying "I think," she used a disclaimer only when her opinion lacked conviction based on data. Stakeholders believed and acted on her results. She had earned their trust. And the painful eye-rolling disappeared.

ACT AFTER A SQUACK SESSION

Make and share your decisions.

You may believe the stakeholders advised you to change your deliverable to match their mental model. Remember, you get to choose which Suggestions to contemplate, to mold into your deliverable, or to ignore.

The decision is yours.

Depending on how formal your organization is you may need to describe how you responded to each Suggestion. More-formal organizations may track every item in a spreadsheet or other project management tool.

If you work in a small or minimally hierarchical organization, you may just need to mentally catalog your reaction (in case the topic comes up again). But, in any case, you are obligated to remember hearing, considering, and making a decision about each Suggestion.

Documenting your decisions throughout the project can cause stressure—stress + pressure. Don't fret. Documentation becomes much more important later, after you've worked through ambiguities and tightened decisions. By that time, you have confidence in your decisions and should feel honored to describe your rationale.

When you need expertise from others to ensure your design gets launched, it's time to document your decisions, explain your design rationale, and capture your responses to Suggestions. Ideally, your transparency will encourage stakeholders to remove obstacles, tackle hurdles, and move mountains to get the design into your customers' hands.

In real life

At Capital One, we set expectations with our stakeholders for how we would track their SQUACK feedback. Our tracking fidelity, like the user experience itself, changed through the project from low to high fidelity. We tracked negligible feedback about our wireframes; but once we conducted our midpoint SQUACK review, our tracking fidelity increased. We then copied each SQUACK item into a shared spreadsheet, whether we collected the feedback via sticky notes or from online chats. We tracked each item with the following columns: the SQUACK category, description, location (either a screen or bubble), decision/action, agent, status, and stakeholder.

We could sort by name and status to know whether one of our Fran Tic or Egoma Niac stakeholders would be on the prowl for how we responded to their feedback. Unfortunately, stakeholders didn't always sign their sticky notes.

In subsequent SQUACK reviews, we proactively thwarted their concerns by announcing our actions, declaring a delay to a future release, or describing why we disregarded their feedback (due to a technical constraint, business decision, lack of supportive User Signal, etc.).

Essentially, we calmed their nerves.

Avoid confirmation bias.

Don't tune your attention to what you want to hear. Digging deeper may spur a conversation that rounds out your own ideas. Suggestions from others can expand your own storytelling, because other people may provide distinctive context about your deliverable.

Consider how the Suggestions could provide more emotional sustenance for your work. If you open yourself up to others' Suggestions, you may leverage emotional storytelling with your rational problem-solving to delight, teach, and nudge your stakeholders and your users alike.

Your stakeholders may steer you toward a new destination and tirelessly remove roadblocks along the path, especially when you're considering their Suggestions.

In real life

Bo Gus, a senior designer, exaggerated the enthusiasm of his stakeholder, Fran Tic: "No surprises. She loved our progress." My observations definitely failed to align with Bo's. Luckily, we could watch the recording of our remote SQUACK session.

First, we turned off the volume and jotted Fran's facial expressions: no smiles, raised eyebrows. Once Bo added the audio, he didn't hear any enthusiasm. Instead, he, too, assessed doubt.

Overly enthusiastic about his own work, Bo had neglected to listen for doubt and failed to paraphrase Fran's Suggestions. Bo reached out to Fran based on our discussion after watching the video. We didn't know whether he needed to repair the relationship; we did know he needed to increase his understanding.

Fran appreciated Bo asking for clarifications and showing he understood the original concerns. Fran's goals and concerns simply stretched beyond Bo's work. Ultimately, Bo and Fran formed a partnership that stretched beyond the original design context, and Bo formed a more realistic appreciation about his own work.

Don't just dismiss Suggestions.

Stakeholder Suggestions may not make sense (to you) or may feel nonessential or more like nice-to-have pleading. You need to explore your stakeholders' Suggestions to uncover what they know or what secrets they are implicitly conveying to you.

So, take the time to first understand and then explore how to accept a Suggestion. You may discover ways to improve your deliverable because your stakeholder has a broader and often different context than you do.

Otherwise, if you ignore stakeholder Suggestions without digging into their context, you may unintentionally spur your stakeholders to dig deeper into your deliverable, scrutinize how you work, or even upgrade their ideas into Critical issues and force you to respond to every single SQUACK comment they make.

In real life

When I shared an idea with my manager at Los Alamos National Laboratory early in my career, she suggested I discuss it with someone I had never met. I didn't see the connection between our tool, which collected resume information from the scientists to create grant proposals, and the head of the nuclear waste management team.

"Really? Isn't he the head of hazardous waste treatment?" I asked coyly.

"Yes," Beth said enthusiastically and with a sheepish grin. "You're not shy; go meet him."

I stopped by his office and showed him the data collection and tracking tool we'd created. I demonstrated how we could manipulate data we collected from every scientist at will for different purposes. Before today's content management systems, our tool was cutting edge. That is, people who worked in software would have been impressed.

If you worked in hazardous waste, you were likely to be more confused than impressed. He reacted kindly, but clearly, the Internet, software, and data collection meant little to his business. I left feeling a bit confused myself; why was Beth so adamant that I speak with him?

Clarity came two months later, when Beth announced her retirement and the division went through a reorganization. In hindsight, I recognized that she urged me to meet him because she knew how important he would be in my career.

Because of Beth's odd prompting, I already knew my new boss and he knew about our work. She had my back, because she had a vantage point that I could not see.

Build offline rapport and amplify your stakeholder's expertise.

Aim to uncover the expertise or pet peeves of each of your stakeholders based on trends in their Suggestions. You may uncover a strength in them where you are weak or identify a fellow expert who can commiserate or imagine with you. Or, even better, you may find someone who can make Suggestions that challenge you to think differently.

You may not uncover the value your stakeholders provide until they have SQUACKed multiple deliverables. Once you understand their strengths, reach out to them individually for an expert review or for guidance to help you strengthen your prowess in that area.

People appreciate showcasing their value and expertise. You may find an opportunity to SQUACK one another's work and amplify everyone's expertise.

In real life

Ami Cable noticed I enjoyed making her content crisper. When I edit, I imagine that every word will cost me $10. I enjoy trimming words as though I'm keeping my friends and myself out of debt.

I amuse myself by diagramming sentences in my head. It's weird. I know. I'm probably rationalizing this habit by making it seem valuable. I imagine dangling on the structure of sentences. When I have time to daydream, I swing on the prepositional trapeze, twisting phrases around to form simpler paths. As I traipse through the sentence, stripping words and phrases, I find the simplest structure that defies the weight of heavy words and complex phrases. It's cathartic, almost aerobic.

Ami's strength, meanwhile, overcame my weakness on this new team. She possessed the historical knowledge of the entire organization. Stakeholders may eventually regret their decisions as policies morph, technology evolves, leadership changes, influence expands, or expertise grows. Ami knew we needed to celebrate the original decisions and investments. She warned when I was too opinionated about an ugly pig. She encouraged me to first applaud the original decisions and then proceed to expertly butcher the swine (not just put lipstick on it).

Essentially, she helped me mend fences before I even knew I had bent them, while I crisped her wording.

Update the context as you conquer decisions and uncover constraints.

When you answer your stakeholders' Questions, ask who else shares their goals to determine whether you need to include those people in your next SQUACK review. When you can understand how your deliverable meets your stakeholders' vision and goals and how those goals are shared among their peers, you may uncover additional stakeholders and can broaden the impact of your deliverable.

Because your FAQ is a living document, add questions and revise your answers as you unearth constraints and discover solutions. You may want to include a tracking date so that your stakeholders can always scan for the latest answers.

In real life

Amazon's Press Release + FAQ tradition, also known as "Working backward from the customer," is documented in *Forbes* and *Harvard Business Review,* and elsewhere. The most important guidance you'll find online is to include essential information in the first six pages and FAQs for customers and internal Amazonians in your appendix.

One comprehensive FAQ answered questions about a new design language for the whole company. It contained the traditional six pages plus more than 80 FAQs.

Exhausting.

Immense.

Massive.

As they socialized the document across the enterprise, the product and UX teams added FAQs. They knew their document so well that they didn't even reference it when someone asked a Question. Instead, they merely said, "That's question #X on page Y." Their confidence expanded by answering every question, in writing.

Don't delay. Fix the Accidents.

If your stakeholders call out an Accident, you are obligated to fix it.

Period.

You will lose credibility and respect if your stakeholders notice the same Accident the next time they SQUACK your work. Seeing a repeated mistake may actually inspire your stakeholders to dive deeper and possibly squawk noisily. They may become suspicious when they think you have become lazy, distracted, or careless.

Remember, they took the time to point out the Accident.

You owe them the time to fix it.

In real life

You may qualify for an exception to the fix-Accidents-before-the-next-SQUACK-review rule if you have a learning disability. My friend Matt Odom, who was a chemist when I was working at Los Alamos National Laboratory, had a brilliant mind that was challenged with dyslexia. He essentially made careless errors (at least that's what other people called them). He proactively mitigated his challenge by auto-correcting words when he typed them backward or when he erroneously substituted one vowel for another. He recognized this inverse pattern and forced his word processor to fix those Accidents automatically.

Matt candidly described his dyslexia. Otherwise, his failure to fix Accidents could have led to apprehension and doubt among his stakeholders, especially when they noted Matt's mistakes multiple times. "As I have yet to conquer the problem completely, being open and honest is a key social tool that gets me through the day!" he explained via chat.

I suspect numerous problems could be mitigated with social connections, honesty, and integrity.

Quietly reflect on the good, the bad, and the worrisome.

After the SQUACK session, recall the feedback process and appreciate your work and the effort from your stakeholders as they expressed their contributions to make your design better.

Appreciate the written, spoken, and implied Kudos about yourself, your team, and your work. Be mindful of the good news and congratulate yourself!

In real life

Reflection apparently isn't as rewarding as it should be. Scientists (*Science*, June 2014) asked research participants if they would be willing to pay money to avoid an electrical shock. Although 100% said they would rather pay than be shocked, 67% of men and 25% of women chose to inflict a shock on themselves rather than just sit and think quietly for 15 minutes.

Yet, being mindful reduces stress, blood pressure, and chronic pain. Decompressing after beating a stressful deadline, working through ambiguity, and creating an original deliverable is precious. Strive to relish those accomplishments.

I decompress by walking stairs after a SQUACK session. Stairwells are surprisingly private. The added incentive to move up or down the steps encourages me to think about the session. If we're working remotely, I do an extra lap around the house. I quietly reflect on ways to improve the process, the collaboration, and the results and where I have earned Kudos. Then I let it all go and, as the slogan says, carry on.

SUMMARY+

Planning a SQUACK session

1. Seek SQUACK long before you have the "right" design.
2. Provide abundant context for the work you'll be SQUACKing. See page 122.
3. Schedule enough time for the length of your deliverable: ~5 minutes per page of a document and ~3 minutes per screen for apps or websites.
4. Prepare to coach your SQUACKers by paraphrasing and categorizing their feedback.
5. Order table tents and posters or download the SQUACK Overview Slide to display during the session from squackfeedback.com.
6. Add large numbers to each page/screen of your design for easy reference.
7. Detach yourself from your work (be proud of the process you followed and the problems you pro-actively prevented).
8. Close the loop with previous SQUACKers regarding unresolved Suggestions or Criticals.

9. Double-check for Accidents and fix any grammatical errors, careless math mistakes, and pixel imperfections.

10. If you're SQUACKing a prototype for a mobile app, enable your SQUACKers to access your designs on their own devices.

11. Savor your previous Kudos.

12. Plan for the logistics of either in-person or remote SQUACK sessions.

    a. In person—Do you need to order pens? Do you have enough sticky notes? Do you need to adjust the colors of the sticky notes based on your inventory? Does your printer have enough paper? Ideally, print and hang the designs in advance. Hang pages across the room (rather than one page above the other). Display the SQUACK formula as a poster or table tent. Do you need a timer?

    b. Remotely—Will all your SQUACKers have digital access to your work? You might pilot your process with friendly SQUACKers before the real session. Will they add SQUACK comments in the same tool you used to create the work or through a chat or shareable document? How will you know when folks are done? Will they put their cursors in a specific spot on the screen? Will they raise their hands in a video conference system? Or will they vote with a thumbs-up in a chat?

Facilitating a SQUACK session

13. Display the SQUACK formula and how to access the work being SQUACKed, ideally throughout the session (not just at the beginning) for people who join late.

14. Acknowledge the whole team for their contributions to your work. Lavish your Kudos for all contributors.

15. Clarify when each SQUACK category is (and is not) helpful according to your team's process (see page 116 for the simplified product life cycle).

16. Remind attendees about the SQUACK formula (either on the poster or table tent in the room or in the meeting invite).

17. Walk through your work at a very high level (avoid describing details that they'll find for themselves).

18. Provide instructions for how to leave SQUACK feedback (sticky notes? interactive chat?).

19. Invite the attendees to read through and SQUACK the work individually (or if it's a prototype for a mobile app, invite them to tap through it).

20. Enjoy being the center of attention, while people SQUACK quietly

21. Invite the group to share any overall SQUACK feedback for the work as a whole.

22. Move to the first screen and work through the SQUACK comments. Typically, one person states all their comments for that page and then the

next person shares theirs, and so on from person to person around the room, without repeating SQUACKs. Or, if you have collected SQUACK comments digitally, you may read through them one-by-one, starting with the first screen.

23. For each item, ask for clarifications as needed. You may not have time to discuss every SQUACK statement, but you do need to ensure that you understand each one. Typically, you'll want to follow this order.

   a. Criticals: Ask for help and action agents to resolve the issue, if needed.

   b. Suggestions: If you can readily agree, let the SQUACKer know you'll act on their Suggestions. For Suggestions you may not accept immediately, express that you'll consider them. Try not to debate the viability of Suggestions, especially if you've already considered them or disagree with them. You may need to prepare a response offline rather than during the SQUACK session.

   c. Questions: Determine whether the Question is intended for you or another person and whether you need to answer now or if you can defer.

   d. Accidents: Remind the SQUACKers that Accidents don't need to be discussed, because you can easily fix them offline.

    e. User Signal: Ask the SQUACKer to translate the research they've heard into either a Suggestion that still needs to be considered or a Kudo with congratulations to the team for solving the user problem.

    f. Kudos: Show appreciation for hearing Kudos.

24. Consider capturing your notes publicly (for example, you could share a spreadsheet digitally with the feedback categories by page; move sticky notes that you plan to act on to an "Action" pile; or share a file with the stakeholders so that they can track your progress). Essentially, show your SQUACKers that you take their input seriously.

25. If your SQUACKers aren't following the formula, categorize their feedback for them and verify that you selected the correct category. Or try a little humor. The SQUACK Collaboration Kit describes several *squeakin' chicken traditions* like squeezing the rubber chicken if a SQUACKer repeats other's feedback or tries to discuss an Accident (see squackfeedback.com for more ideas and to purchase the kit).

26. Establish shared next steps and timelines.

27. Adjourn by giving Kudos to the attendees for SQUACKing. Be sincere about how using the SQUACK formula clarifies the actions you need to take.

Acting after a SQUACK session

28. Act on the SQUACK feedback: consider every Suggestion, update your FAQ with new Questions and answers, determine whether more User Signal is merited, fix the Accidents, seek help removing obstacles and constraints to resolve the Criticals, and archive the Kudos.

29. Identify any trends in the Accidents and determine whether you can proactively eliminate them. Do you need help with grammar and punctuation? Do you need to establish a design component library to avoid inconsistencies?

30. Track and share the status of how you're responding to the SQUACK feedback, especially for Critical issues and feedback received later in the life cycle.

31. Quietly reflect on any good, bad, or worrisome trends in the SQUACK feedback.

32. Build offline rapport with your stakeholders and amplify their expertise.

33. Invent self-Kudos about the value you put into the work and the expertise you gained along the way.

OH, THE PLACES YOU'LL SQUACK

Remember, Amazon maxed out at 5,000 books about feedback and Google offered more than 621 million search results. Feedback is definitely used beyond UX deliverables. SQUACK can help us clarify feedback in the doctor's office, with our romantic partners, and when collaborating with other disciplines.

Follow what the doctor SQUACKed.

According to an article published in *Reuters Health* in November 2017, a typical consultation between a patient and their primary care physician in the United States lasts only 20 minutes. In fact, doctors typically spend just 12-17% of their day with patients. The remainder is spent on processing forms, reviewing lab results, dealing with other staff members, and updating medical files.

As patients, SQUACK can potentially help us optimize our appointment by ensuring our physicians answer our Questions, we understand their Suggestions and know how to act on any Critical advice. Otherwise, we may leave the office with mounds of ideas, but little clarity.

In real life

In my experience, diabetes educators enthusiastically share ideas, expertise, anecdotes, and advice about nutrition, exercise, basal insulin, bolus insulin, diet, and carbohydrates.

I arrived at a recent appointment inspired. I wanted to do a better job monitoring the disease I've had since childhood. But the options felt overwhelming.

I would have to change my entire regimen.

My life.

I felt skepticism and resentment seep into the conversation between the educator, my husband, Robert, and me.

Then I had a SQUACK moment.

I simply asked her to focus on what was Critical from all the advice she could give me. It was a changing point.

She reflected and considered.

Listened to me.

And gave me the number-one change I needed to make.

Great. I could handle that one thing.

Deciphering that one piece of Critical health advice from the numerous Suggestions made me much more receptive to adjusting my routine.

Quit squabbling with your partner: start SQUACKing.

I don't claim to be a marriage counselor or a therapist, but I've heard from multiple SQUACKers that SQUACK works at home with their partners. Every night, Zoe Yang asks her husband, Jason, to "Please start with the Kudos, honey, then tell me your Suggestions." They have drawn out S-Q-U-A-C-K on a white board in their kitchen to help them categorize and reflect.

In real life

I've also used SQUACKed with my husband, a retired sales executive. If I didn't, our marriage couldn't have survived five home remodels in 20 years. Afterall, the top reasons for divorce typically include infidelity, financial squabbles, and fighting during a home renovation. SQUACK can help minimize the strain and emphasize what's actually important to prevent wrecked restorations and relationships (not sure it can help minimize the other reasons for divorce).

Robert has been our general contractor, so he's heard tons of 3 W's (Worries, Wants, and Wishes) from me over the years. We're both talkers and problem solvers. I've learned that when I emphatically want something updated, I need to designate the improvement as Critical.

And he's learned when to get my attention with a Critical to mitigate obstacles or make a choice urgently. Distinguishing Criticals from Suggestions is imperative for us.

Your mileage may vary.

You SQUACK my doc, I'll SQUACK yours.

Critique sessions in design school can feel intentionally brutal and emotionally draining. One faculty member shared that her critiques are intended to help students build thick skin. If her students lack talent and resiliency, they quickly abandon design school for another career path. Her design crits deliberately separate the frightened students from the fierce.

She's not alone in this mindset. The art school critiques teach designers across specialties to shrug and carry on.

Once they enter the workforce, designers will likely interact with peers who have not faced humiliating critiques. These peers may deliberately shun feedback sessions about their deliverables.

During a "You SQUACK my doc, I'll SQUACK yours" session, the designers offer to hear SQUACK feedback about their own work. They model how to react nondefensively, answering the Questions they can, considering Suggestions, asking for help to resolve Criticals, fixing Accidents, and graciously accepting Kudos.

They then model how to provide SQUACK feedback to the other disciplines. They show vulnerability about their own work, concern about other people, and a willingness to improve their own and their peer's work. The key is to remind the recipients that they own what, if anything, to do with the Suggestions and recognize that feedback is not about them. SQUACK concerns the deliverable, not the person.

In real life

Our marketing counterparts at one financial services company lived, breathed, and dreamed about the brand tone and style. They had the history, tribal knowledge, and foresight for the future of the brand as we evolved the experience and the products digitally. I had expertise in writing for user interfaces—crisp, clear, and direct. We wrote to make the users succeed. Our marketing partners wrote to protect the brand.

Compromising on style and tone would please neither discipline.

Rather, I took an approach to share feedback on each team's core deliverables. I asked my branding partners to SQUACK the rubrics for our UI style guide and urged them to permit me to augment the brand style guide from a UX perspective.

Then, once we elaborated on the style rules, we did a gut check and reviewed a writing example by each discipline. The original marketing message, for a banner ad, had 300+ characters. My Suggestions emphasized the principle that online users were unlikely to read the full banner. My marketing partners emphasized the text needed to appeal to the full spectrum of customers, since we were not personalizing the experience by segment.

Eventually, we established a content team, composed of UI designers and marketing content writers, to SQUACK content together. The team held shared office hours where they would SQUACK proposed content together. Eventually, they gravitated toward a shared style guide as each team member embraced the purpose of the other discipline. The embrace and appreciation did not occur immediately; but the disciplines did learn to appreciate the other point-of-view and recognized content could be both usable and on-brand.

In other words, little by little, a new design style and tone emerged, thanks to the collaborative nature of SQUACK.

Be the first to try a SQUACK-a-thon.

I haven't tried a SQUACK-a-thon yet, but if you do, maybe we'll publish your *In real life* anecdote.

I imagine makers across all disciplines sharing their work in any fidelity and getting SQUACK feedback to help refine it.

Makers could sign up for a timeslot with an estimate of how long the session should take (rule of thumb: 5 minutes per page if a document and 3 minutes per screen if an app). The intent would be to openly seek informal feedback in a structured, actionable format.

Maybe it could even be a more social event, where any maker outcome is SQUACKed, not just work-related concepts.

Are you in?

I'd love to hear about it at squackfeedback.com.

SQUACK the boat beyond UX.

With an estimated 2.5 quintillion bytes of data created every day, only a fraction can be analyzed. No wonder data scientist is one of the biggest career opportunities. "We need math, statistics, an openness to hack, and patience to test and test again," said Zoe Yang, former Director of Data Science at Capital One. "It's a team sport, which means that data scientists need to collect feedback from other team members. We wrangle data, generate questions, form hypotheses, score our evidence, build a model, and rank our confidence."

Once possible answers are created, data scientists score them.

These verbs—analyze, wrangle, generate, form, build, and rank—are maker verbs.

Data scientists crave the SQUACK feedback formula, too. "SQUACK simplifies our hacking process," Zoe explained. "Our algorithms, models, and dashboards can be SQUACKed like any design or product deliverable."

Take stock of your SQUACK tools.

You may find that your team's interest and practice of SQUACK wanes over time. No worries. The following resources can help you sustain the momentum:

- Business cards with the SQUACK formula
- Table tents for conference rooms
- Downloadable images that you can add to your presentations and documents
- Posters
- Excel templates for tracking your SQUACK action items

These resources are available at squackfeedback.com. We are constantly looking for other ways to help people and teams tackle mental hurdles. Our goal is to unleash your creativity and enhance collaboration.

APPLAUSE TO BETA SQUACKERS & OTHER CONTRIBUTORS

Amanda Culver who nonchalantly mentioned during a UX-book-of-the-month discussion that when she reads a page of instructions, she only really understands when she hears a real-world story. Amanda, you unknowingly reinforced the approach I wanted to take for this book. Thank you for the real User Signal!

Audrey Doyle, the copywriter who reminded me about grammar gurus. Thanks for pushing me to say more with fewer words.

Aurea Calvo Almeida for being a beta SQUACKer extraordinaire. Thank you for your branding advice and counsel.

Barbara Rigg-Healey, my manager at the UNM Computer and Information Technology Center, for the opportunity and encouragement to take a risk as an undergraduate editor. Thanks for tolerating the chaos,

Barbara, when I figured out how to integrate that document.

Colleen Sheehan, book designer, who expanded my explorations, made sense of stream-of-consciousness, and tamed the Albatross. Thanks for making these books worthy of shelf space.

Dario Figueroa who forced me to buy domains! Thanks always for the challenge.

Danielle Goodman, the developmental editor who convinced me I had three audiences and three books. Thanks for tripling my work!

David Scaliatine who formatted a SQUACK definition slide that beautifully emphasized the definitions. I appreciate you taking the time to share your thoughts in the Foreward, too. You were working, going to school, and writing. Thanks.

Eddy Escalier who took my favorite headshot photo. (I know you credit the subdued sunlight in Seattle, but I value your expertise. Besides, who would ever believe there are sunny days in Seattle?).

Gail Tomiak who texted me when she found a Kudos note I gave her 15+ years ago. Thanks for reminding me about the importance of sharing gratitude (and making people laugh).

Kevin Dewey who volunteered as my first beta SQUACKer. Thank you for kicking me into making the book real.

Kevin Domingo for the inspirational doodle of the SQUACKing birds. I appreciate your visualization skills and ability to capture the essence of the formula so effectively.

Larissa Scordato for improving my approach to diversity and inclusiveness. Your detailed advice proved immensely helpful.

Logan Theodore for helping to refine the remote capabilities of SQUACK with a willingness to jump in and explore.

Sunjay Pandey for introducing me to so many Seattle coffee shops where we debated, discussed, and dared to do the right thing. Thanks for your wise counsel and allyship.

Susan Price for your continued willingness to listen to my aspirations and occasionally kick me to go make them happen. I truly appreciate your strategic out-of-the-box thinking.

Susan Todd for your thoughtful yet blunt, candid, and on-target feedback. You are a User Signal guru.

Tricia Adams for all-around great SQUACK advice. You're adept at transitioning from generalist to specialist and back. I truly appreciate your adaptive capabilities. Brussels sprouts soon?

Zoe Yang for being an all-around great sport and partner. Milk tea soon?

Last but foremost, Kudos to my husband, **Robert,** for your not-ever-subtle Suggestions about 5 homes, 5 dogs, and 1 pack of wolves. I really appreciate the real you.

GLOSSARY & INDEX

Kudos archive – A digital or physical stash of praise and appreciation that you collect over time. Reference your archive when the imposter syndrome or doubts are lurking, especially when you've heard negative feedback or hurtful opinions. The archive can remind you of your value, expertise, and accomplishments. Page 108.

Simplified product life cycle – Because organizations need processes based on their own preferences, priorities, and procedures, I abridged the essential steps required to deliver quality designs to customers to 1. explore needs, 2. revise the design, 3. develop the code, and 4. launch to customers. The type of SQUACK feedback needed and appreciated for each step is described on Page 116.

SQUACK – A neologism based on categorizing feedback to make it actionable. The feedback categories are S for Suggestion, Q for Question, U for User Signal, A for Accident, C for Critical and K for Kudos. Page 2.

UXer – Design, research, or writing professionals who create assets for end users and likely collect feedback from peers, partners, managers, and stakeholders.

WARTS – The weaknesses, adaptations, risks, tradeoffs, and shortcomings that typically influence every piece of work. I recommend being transparent and seeking help to eliminate or reduce the size of the WARTS. Page 21, 46, 63, 97, 122, 125.

Made in United States
Orlando, FL
01 May 2022